Growing In . . . the Word

Neil T. Anderson
Alistair Begg
Steve Chalke
Jim Cymbala
Mike DiSanza and Liz Hinds
Nick Fawcett
Malcolm Folley
Melody Green
Jill Gupta
Wayne Kirkland
Tim LaHaye and Jerry B. Jenkins
Peter Lewis
Bridget Plass
R.C. Sproul
Tommy Tenney

Copyright © 2001 SAM BOOKS

First published in 2001 by SAM BOOKS

Permissions have been granted by the following publishers:
Baker Book House
The Bible Reading Fellowship
HarperCollins*Publishers*
Harvest House Publishers
Hodder & Stoughton
Inter-Varsity Press
Kingsway Publications
Kevin Mayhew Limited
Monarch Books
Moody Press
OM Publishing
Scripture Union
Thomas Nelson, Inc
Tyndale House Publishers, Inc.
Zondervan Publishing House
Full copyright details are included at the beginning of each chapter

05 04 03 02 01   7 6 5 4 3 2

British Library Cataloguing in Publication Data
A catalogue record for this book is available from the British Library
ISBN 1-900836-12-2

Cover Design by Philip Houghton, Carlisle
Typeset by WestKey Ltd, Falmouth
Printed by Ebner, Ulm

Contents

Foreword

"It is a good book that is opened with expectation,
and closed with delight and profit."

No excuse should really be necessary to pick up and read a good book. Yet all too often we need a prompt to encourage us to spend our valuable time with a book.

World Book Day is a worldwide celebration of books and reading and an ideal opportunity to present a selection of some of the best, newly published Christian titles.

Brought together under one cover, fiction rubs shoulders with eschatology, biography with theology, prayers with suffering and victorious living. As with the one true good book, God's word the Bible, Christian writers cover a rich diversity of subjects and themes – from birth to death, contemporary issues, inspiring lives, timeless truths.

May 'Growing in the Word' this World Book Day give you an excuse to dig deeper into God's Word, draw nourishment from the experiences of others, and bear fruit for the kingdom.

Debbie Bunn,
Editor, *Challenge Magazine*

A Cop for Christ

Mike DiSanza and Liz Hinds

Officer Mike DiSanza of the New York Police Department was a cop just like any other, when a near-death experience led to an amazing turnaround in his perception of the world. He discovered a new message of hope and compassion for all of God's people and a new call on his own career.

Mike's is a dramatic story. Growing up in the Bronx, he spent more than twenty-two gritty years with the NYPD. His astonishing ministry takes the love of Jesus to people who know life only as a struggle for survival.

Mike DiSanza is President of International Cops for Christ.

Hodder & Stoughton
ISBN: 0-340-78519-5

Price: £5.99

£4.99 with money off voucher

First published in 2001 by Hodder & Stoughton
A Division of Hodder Headline Ltd
338 Euston Road
London NW1 3BH

Chapter 1

I was ready for him. I stood with my knees slightly bent, my body angled towards my opponent and a piece of wood gripped firmly in my hands.

'You're going to have to do better than that, Charlie, if you wanna get me outta here,' I yelled.

'Just you wait, Mikey, see what you can do with this.'

'Oh yeah? Come on, then.'

I grinned. Let him try, I thought. I was ten years old. I had all the confidence in the world.

At the other end of the concrete school-yard, Charlie began his pitch, his face distorted with determination. His last ball had hit the wall behind my knees, well outside the large chalk square that represented home plate, but this time he was sure he was going to get a strike, I knew it. And I was just as determined to stop him.

Charlie completed his pitch. His timing was perfect. The small rubber Spading ball shot through the air straight towards the large chalk square ... and straight towards the old broomhandle I was using as a bat. I drew it back and swung it forward to hit the Spading, which soared high into the sky. I put up my hand to shield my eyes from the sun as I watched the ball's progress. Charlie turned and was watching it too, as he started to run, following the line through the air, hoping to make a catch. Our eyes continued to follow the ball as it started its descent. Charlie speeded up and then came to a sudden halt. His way was blocked by the solid brick wall of the old catholic church which bordered one side of the school-yard. The ball landed on the roof and bounced into the guttering.

I walked over to join Charlie, and we stood together and looked up at the roof. We'd pooled our money to buy the ball the day before. It was the only ball we had, and we had no more money.

'We gotta get it back.'

'Yeah' Charlie agreed.

'Look, if you give me a shimmy, I should be able to get up there. It's not too high.'

We walked along beside the wall, studying it until we found the most likely-looking section with the most footholds, and then Charlie bent over and formed his hands into a cradle. I put my left foot in, then felt around the rough brickwork of the wall until I found an edge I could grip. With Charlie pushing and me pulling myself up, I could just reach the edge of the flat rooftop. I gave it a tug to test its safety.

'It's okay, it'll hold me. Just give me another bunk up.'

Down below, Charlie grunted. It was a hot day. I could hear him take a deep breath and then he straightened up as far as he could, supporting my weight. It was enough. With a final heave I pulled myself up on to the roof, and what I saw there, I tell you, I would have given a plate of my mother's meatballs for.

'Charlie, gold!' I yelled.

'What? What you talking about, Mikey?'

'Here, catch, Charlie.'

One by one, and then two by two, I showered Charlie with balls, the legacy of generations of kids who'd played softball in the school-yard. We'd stumbled across treasure.

'Wow!'

I sent Charlie scuttling all over the place collecting up the balls that I bounced down from above, until at last the roof was clear. We must have had at least a hundred balls. I scrambled down and we hunted around until we found a box to store them in. When we'd done, we stood back and looked at our plunder. There were enough balls there to last all summer at least. We grinned at each other and then, suddenly, Charlie remembered something.

'Hey, the ball went out of play so that means you're out.'

I was about to argue with him when we heard the squeal of the school-yard gate opening. We looked around. There were two gangs, one black, one white, of youths coming into the yard. We didn't know what was going on but it didn't look good. We hurriedly pushed our box into a corner behind a shed and crouched down beside it.

When the yard was full – there must have been two hundred there altogether – one of the youths took a heavy metal chain and padlocked the gate. We knew then that whatever was happening, no one was going to leave until it was over.

The rival gangs lined up on opposite sides of the yard, and there was a nervous silence. The air smelled of sweat and fear. Then two of the older youths strode into the centre of the yard. They each raised an arm and held it in the air for a moment before dropping it. This must have been the signal the rest were waiting for. The two gangs charged. They laid into each other using knives, chains, baseball bats, the sharp pointed metal of car aerials, or anything they had been able to lay their hands on that would cause damage to their enemy.

Charlie and I cowered in the corner, huddled together, watching all this, not daring to move or say a word, thankful that no one had spotted us.

After what seemed like hours but was probably only ten minutes, we heard the sound of sirens wailing as police cars approached the yard. We figured some passers-by must have seen the fight and called the police. The gang members heard the sirens too, over the screaming and yelling, and those that could still walk struggled to climb over the chain-link fence to escape. Others were too badly injured to get up off the ground, where they lay bleeding or semi-conscious.

When it was all over and the last body had been taken away in an ambulance or a squad car, Charlie and I stood up. We didn't say anything, just picked up the box of balls between us and made our way slowly back home.

That incident, my first real encounter with violence, had a profoundly shocking effect on me. For three months afterwards I shut myself away, refusing to leave the apartment. I went straight to school in the morning and came straight home again at night. My mom and dad couldn't understand it.

They asked me, 'What's the matter with you, Mike?'

But I didn't want to talk about it, I couldn't talk about it. Charlie and I had seen the kind of things no one should see when they're only ten years old.

The balls, the treasure we had found, stayed unused in their box that summer.

Perhaps Charlie and I were lucky to have reached ten years old without witnessing violence, living as we did in New

York's notorious South Bronx. While the majority of people who lived there were families like mine and Charlie's, decent hard-working men and women who struggled to give their children a good upbringing in spite of poverty and bad conditions, there were others who chose a different life, and what Charlie and I had seen that day was an everyday part of life for many.

But not for us.

I was born in the South Bronx in 1946 to Albert and Bernadette DiSanza. They'd both been born in New York City of immigrant parents. My mom was Italian and my dad was Spanish–Italian. Economically we were at the bottom of the scale. My dad had had to leave school during the Depression, and both my parents worked in factories for very little pay. My mom was a seamstress in a sweatshop. They were hard workers but they only earned enough money to keep us fed and for the bare essentials. We were a typical Italian–Spanish family: we ate lots of spaghetti, which was cheap, and my mom's meatballs, which were the best. We didn't have a car or a television, but we had a good loving home.

The six of us – my parents, me, my twin brother Thomas, my older brother John and my little sister Laura – lived on the fifth, the top floor of an apartment building on 148th Street. In any street on the Bronx, there are maybe ten buildings on each side, each building housing thirty families. My grandparents had ten children and they all lived on the same street, so I was never short of cousins to play with.

The neighbourhood we lived in was predominantly Italian. If a family moved out, it was usually another Italian family that would move in. The Bronx was like that, split into ethnic areas. As well as the Italian quarter, there were black, Irish and Puerto Rican neighbourhoods.

Coming from a Roman Catholic family, I grew up

attending St Peter's, the local Catholic church. Roman Catholicism and all its rituals played a large part in my early life. We went to confession on Saturdays and Mass on Sundays. There seemed to be rules and regulations governing everything I did. I soon learned that if I did wrong and died without making confession, I would go to hell, and that it was a terrible, terrible place. This was drummed into me and the fear of it overwhelmed me; it was always there in the back of my mind. The only way to avoid going to hell was to go to confession, and that became part of my Saturday ritual.

Like any normal kid I was constantly doing wrong during the week, and it was a real worry for me that I would have an accident and die before I had a chance to confess my sins the next Saturday.

One of the many rules I learned by heart was that it was a sin to eat meat on Fridays.

Every Sunday we'd have meatballs for dinner. My mom worked of a Saturday so she'd prepare the meatballs on Friday and freeze them – that way they'd be ready and she wouldn't have to spend a long time making them on Sunday. One day I got home from school and found that she had forgotten to put the meatballs in the freezer. Instead, she'd left them out on the kitchen table. I looked at the tray of meatballs and my mouth watered. My moms meatballs were so good.

'She won't miss it,' I told myself, 'if I just take one.

I put out my hand towards the tray, then I stopped.

'Nah, I shouldn't.'

I turned away, but the delicious smell filling the kitchen stopped me. I looked over my shoulder at the meatballs. I'm sure I heard them call out to me – surely it wouldn't hurt if I just took one?

I grabbed the juiciest-looking and stuffed it in my mouth. Mmm, it tasted good. But now there was a gap on the tray where my meatball had been. I figured if I moved the others around a bit no one would notice there was one missing, and I was just wiping my hands when I remembered something.

It was Friday.

A sudden cold fear gripped my stomach.

I wasn't supposed to eat meat on Fridays.

I knew if my mom found out that I'd taken a meatball she would shout at me, but she'd soon forgive me. I wasn't scared about that. No, I was scared because I'd committed a far more serious sin – the sin of eating meat on a Friday. I knew that if I died that night I'd go to hell, and just because of that one meatball. I didn't sleep that night and I was first in line for confession the next day.

When I got older, I liked to go out on the town on Saturday nights with the boys. After one Saturday night when we'd been drinking and partying, I overslept. When I woke up, I rolled over in my bed and looked at the clock. I saw it was early afternoon. I closed my eyes again and then suddenly I sat bolt upright, wide awake.

'I've missed Mass!'

The thought struck me like a thunderbolt from heaven. I'd missed Mass and that was a mortal sin. If I died before going to confession next Saturday, I would go to hell.

I couldn't go back to sleep now. I sat on the edge of the bed, trying to calm the anxious thoughts going round my head. I wondered if a hot bath would make me feel better. I got up, went to the bathroom and turned on the faucet (water tap). When the bath was full enough, I dipped my hand in to test the temperature.

'Ow!' I pulled my hand out quickly. I hadn't turned

on the cold water and the bath was scalding hot. That was when it hit me. If I can't take this hot water for one second, how am I going to cope with burning for ever in hell?

I changed my mind about the bath. Instead, I pulled on some clothes and ran down the road to the rectory. I knocked impatiently on the door. When the priest opened it, he was rubbing his eyes, looking like he'd just been woken up from his Sunday afternoon nap. I blurted out, 'You gotta hear my confession, Father.'

'Why, what's the problem, Mikey? Have you killed someone?'

'No, Father, but I missed Mass this morning.'

'Is that all? Can't you wait until next Saturday to have your confession?'

'It's all right for you. If you die today, you're going to heaven. If I die today, I'm going to hell.'

This was a real concern for me. I was coming to think of God, if he existed at all, as someone who was out to get me. I had no security, no peace, no certainty of my salvation. As far as I was concerned, I was destined for hell, and there was nothing I could do about it. I was a yo-yo Christian, headed for heaven one day and hell the next. The Church told me what to do and what not to do. I knew I could never hit the mark. I was fed up with struggling and always failing, so I stopped going to confession as often.

The next time I went I began, 'Father, forgive me for I have sinned. It has been six months since my last conf–'

The words weren't out of my mouth before the good father was at my side in the confessional. He grabbed me by the shoulders and shook me.

'You didn't come here for six months?!'

I was taken by surprise by his response, but by then I had

lost most of my respect for the Church so I stood up to him.

'No, I haven't been here for six months, and let me tell you why. I'm tired of coming here every week saying the same things and nothing ever changing, so I figured I'd just save it all up for six months, do it all in one go.

The priest looked at me and his face changed. He smiled, 'Well, at least someone round here is honest!'

I often wondered what the priest thought when he listened to confessions on a Saturday. Did the idea of a young boy's stolen meatball make him chuckle? Did he ever question the rules that brought such fear into lives? Did he have any idea what guilt and anxiety were being instilled by the regulations, or what condemnation people were living under?

Eventually I gave up even on the six-monthly confessions. I stopped going to church altogether.

A Time to Jump

Malcolm Folley

Olympic champion, world record holder, dedicated athlete, family man, Christian. This exciting biography charts Jonathan's struggle to reach the top in his sporting career and the challenges to his faith he has overcome.

He talks with candour and warmth about his sporting highs and lows and his spiritual journey thus far.

'My aspiration is to have "walked the walk" and I invite you to judge whether it is a hope that is able to bear the scrutiny of biography.' Malcolm Folley, Chief Sports Reporter for *The Mail on Sunday*, has worked as a sports writer on national newspapers for twenty-five years.

HarperCollins*Publishers*
ISBN: 0-00-274072-9

Price: £6.99

£5.99 with money off voucher

First published in Great Britain in 2001
by HarperCollins*Publishers*

Chapter 3

Never on a Sunday?

Most people are bothered by those passages in Scripture which they cannot understand; but as for me, I have noticed that the passages that trouble me most are the ones I do understand.

Mark Twain

The fresh-faced, skinny student looked incongruous standing by the sandpit wearing a long raincoat over his street clothes. As other young athletes drawn from all over the country careered into the pit, the kid in the coat assisted coach John Crotty in measuring their jumps.

At lunchtime the teenager wrapped up against the chill wind that whips through the Crystal Palace Stadium in winter, picked up his bag and went to King's Cross Station. Ahead of him was a long journey back to Durham University. Those taking part in the training weekends at Crystal Palace in the mid-eighties could never have supposed that one day the kid in the coat would be the best triple jumper the world had ever seen.

Jonathan Edwards volunteered to help with the measuring on Sunday mornings when he was called to London for weekend training with the elite squad that used to assemble under the watchful eye of Crotty. The reason for this was simple: Edwards resolutely refused to train, or for that matter study, on Sundays. He was being consistent with his schooldays, with his upbringing in a household where his father and mother instructed their three children to observe Sunday as a day reserved for worship and time together as a family. No organized ball games, no television, no academic work.

Crotty had watched Edwards win the triple jump in the National Schools Championship in 1984 and invited him to attend national squad training at Crystal Palace the following year. 'The difficulty with Jon was that he didn't always do a lot!' says Crotty dryly. Edwards still calls him on the telephone to this day, specifically if he wants a trained eye to analyse his technique. Crotty possesses a large video library, often shot with his own camera, and he has much footage of Edwards dating back to his earliest competitions.

'Let me give you an example of Jonathan's programme when he came down to Crystal Palace in those days when he was a student at Durham,' Crotty continues. 'He would arrive on Friday night, more often than not going to bed early at the hostel. The next morning he would stretch a bit, jog a bit, but he was very fragile and we had to be careful with him. He was very quick and he had lots of potential, you could see that. He was springy and fast, but at that time he didn't have the endurance strength to train for the triple jump, let alone compete. On the Saturday morning we would do technical work because you need to be at your freshest to do that kind of work. Usually, after about three jumps Jonathan had had enough; he was aching somewhere. So, in the afternoon he would do very little. We would do a number of tests as a group, like a sprint test. Jonathan was always polite, always nice, and he would come and say, "Can't quite make this today, not quite up to it."

We'd play some volleyball later. In the evening we used to play a lot of cards – I'm quite a gambler. Of course, Jonathan was polite, but he never played. He read his Bible and looked after himself. Don't get me wrong, he mixed with everybody, he got on well with everybody, but he had time for himself and we respected that. But the next day was the best day from my point of view ... and looking back you still have to giggle. Of course, Jonathan didn't do anything on a Sunday!' Except pace the sandpit in his raincoat.

Edwards' position was clearly entrenched, at least then. Still, he had no idea of the commotion ahead.

Edwards recalls that he first rebuffed the international selectors by rejecting an invitation to compete for an England A team because the match was being staged on a Sunday. He would not attract nationwide attention, however, until the day he declared that he would miss the trials to determine the team the British selectors would send to the Olympic Games in Seoul in the autumn of 1988. Olympic Games or no Olympic Games, Edwards would not compete in trials that were to be held on a Sunday. His faith, his dedication to be a servant of God, was more important than any athletic ambition.

Edwards recollects that one Sunday afternoon, as a sports-mad schoolboy, he was at a friend's house watching televised football highlights on a programme called *The Big Match* when his father came to fetch him home. Reverend Edwards denies this, chuckling. Yet he explains the sanctity in which Sunday was held within his house. 'I don't remember ever having to go and get Jonathan, but it would be fair to say that we thought Sunday was a day of rest, a day that was unlike any other day of the week; he says. 'Sunday was to be kept as a holy day to be used for family time, to be given for worship. From that point of view we wouldn't do anything which we could normally do in the rest of the week' One of Jonathan's vivid memories is of watching his mother peel and prepare the vegetables for Sunday lunchtime on Saturday evening.

Tim Edwards confirms that with his brother he would 'try to get a sneak look at television if Mum and Dad were in the kitchen'. He explains a typical Sunday in the Edwards household: 'Church, big dinner, Dad would have a rest and perhaps we would take a family walk. Sometimes it was boring!'

Jonathan would later appreciate the value of his parents' position. 'As I got older, it became a very positive thing, I believed this was right: he argues. 'If I had an exam on a Monday, I wouldn't revise on a Sunday. That was it. Jesus, when he healed on the Sabbath, said to the Pharisees, "Sabbath is made for man, not man for the Sabbath." It's a day given to man as a gift, a rest'

Jill Edwards, rightly so, is unapologetic about how her children were taught to observe Sunday, but she says now, With hindsight, I look back and think we were probably more rigid than we needed to have been. But you also have to see where we were coming from that was our background from the time that we were converted. That was very much the era when people didn't do anything on a Sunday. I mean, Sunday sport...' Basically, sports fixtures were not held on a Sunday back then.

At the time when the British trials for the 1988 Olympic Games were scheduled for a Sunday, Edwards was completely certain of the course of action he had to adopt. He would not jump. He was 22 years old and working by day as a scientific officer in the cytogenetics laboratory of the Royal Victoria Infirmary in Newcastle, where he analysed chromosomes for diagnostic purposes. By night he was training at the Gateshead Stadium. He had already jumped the Olympic qualifying standard (16.65 metres) that summer and had jumped the furthest of any British athlete prior to the trials, but apart from catching the eye of those who read the small print of the athletics press Edwards had competed almost anonymously. Until now.

Suddenly, he was being portrayed in nationwide stories as a modern-day Eric Liddell, the man whose fabled stance of placing his religion before his sport had been the inspiration for the Oscar-winning film *Chariots of Fire*. Somewhat predictably, Edwards had not seen the film as his life in North Devon had revolved almost exclusively around school, church and sport when the film was released in 1980. However, millions had seen the movie and had been entranced, and for journalists there was too much of a parallel to ignore between Liddell's principled boycott of the 100 metres race at the 1924 Olympic Games in Paris and Edwards' decision to imperil his hopes of going to the Seoul Olympics in 1988.

One writer called Jean Rafferty graphically encapsulated the spirit Edwards had engendered as she suggested,

A religious athlete is a contradiction in terms in our psyched up, hyped up, drugged up days of sport. Eric Liddell, of Chariots of Fire fame, was already an anachronism when he refused to compete on a Sunday in the Paris Olympic Games. But that was 1924 when there were still a few Christians left in Britain. They have become an endangered species who surprise the rest of us with their eccentric belief in God and the soul and other such things you can't buy with a credit card. Jonathan

Edwards might as well be a time traveller, hundreds of years old, who's come along in his personal Tardis to shake things up a bit.[1]

Edwards was overwhelmed by the fuss. If the trials had been on any other day, he would have jumped. As they were on a Sunday, he would not – as his coach Carl Johnson informed the selectors on his behalf. There was nothing sinister in his decision, nothing pre-planned, no attempt to hijack publicity. He knew that the rules of selection guaranteed places on the Olympic team to the athletes who finished first and second at the trials. He would take his chances of being offered the third, discretionary place. This was a matter of principle, no more, no less.

Besides, he was not alone. Barrington Williams declined to compete in the long jump because that event at the Olympics was scheduled to be staged on a Sunday. Instead Williams, a lay preacher for the Elim Pentecostal Free Church in Chesterfield, Derbyshire, made himself available for the 100 metres. Williams made the Olympics in his alternative event. 'In athletic terms Barrington was a total enigma,' says Edwards. 'His story was amazing, it was the stuff of schoolboy comics:

Williams was a wonderful, colourful character, but Edwards as the younger man was the athlete who caught the imagination of the country. In explanation of his unwillingness to compete in the trials, Edwards said at the time, 'I see my Christian life as the most important thing and I realize I have to make certain sacrifices. I was brought up in a Christian family and happen to believe the Sabbath is holy. I will watch the trials on television and think, "I

---

1 *Plus* magazine, 31 January 1990.

could have been there," but it's just one of those things. It wasn't a difficult decision not to compete. My Christian beliefs are much more important to me than athletics. Some of my friends think I'm foolish. They say I'm throwing away my chances of getting to the Olympics. But I feel this has given me a chance to demonstrate the sincerity of my Christian beliefs and to show to other people just how important Christianity is. I will get another chance. Athletics is not everything to me, but my faith is. I hope that God will repay me in the same way that I have repaid him and I stick to my decision even if it means missing out on the Olympics'

It was little wonder that the media should want to present Edwards as a throwback to Liddell. Of course, the Scotsman was among the favourites to win gold at the Paris Games, while Edwards would have been the first to confirm that any expectations he might take on the plane to Seoul would not extend much beyond walking out in the opening ceremony. Edwards was in the rookie phase; Liddell, who won seven caps on the wing for the Scotland rugby team, was already an outstanding athlete.

Liddell, like Edwards the son of a clergyman, would have been selected for the 100 metres and 200 metres at those Olympic Games in Paris, as well as the two relay teams. But once he discovered that the heats for the 100 metres were to be held on a Sunday (contrary to the screenwriters' licence in the Hollywood version, he knew that before he caught the boat for France) Liddell withdrew from that event. His religious convictions would not allow him to compete on the Sabbath, and through the scheduling of the Games this meant that he also had to excuse himself from the relay squads. Instead, he entered the 400 metres, an event at which he was a relative novice.

The 100 metres was won at the Stade de Colombes on 7 July 1924 by the Englishman Harold Abrahams who, controversially for the times, employed a professional coach, Sam Mussabini. Twenty-four years later Abrahams, who had been to Repton and Cambridge, wrote poignantly, 'I have often wondered whether I owe my Olympic success, at any rate in part, to Eric's religious beliefs. Had he run in that event, would he have defeated me and won the Olympic title?' In the event, Liddell did defeat Abrahams in the Olympic 200 metres final, the Scotsman winning the bronze medal as the Englishman laboured home sixth.

Abrahams' success in the 100 metres was a prominent part of the plot of *Chariots of Fire*, but the central, heart-wrenching theme was Liddell's eventual triumph. Abrahams' account of the Olympic 400 metres final race – and his eulogy – is worth recounting:

I remember that as the seats allotted to Olympic competitors were in a very unfavourable position – at the start of the 100m – I paid my ten shillings (50p) to have a seat near the finish. Liddell was drawn in the outside lane, which meant that he had to make all his own running. The 400m in Paris was run round two bends only, that is to say there was a starting straight of, I should think, very nearly 200 yards. From the crack of the pistol Liddell ran like a man inspired. Indeed, the thought in my mind as he started off as if he was running 100 metres instead of 400, was 'He can't possibly keep this up' But Eric never seemed to slacken in his pace, though of course he must have slowed appreciably, and he won that glorious Olympic final by a good six yards in the new Olympic and world record time of 47.6 seconds.

His name will for ever remain as perhaps the most famous and most respected and loved athlete Scotland has ever produced. His style was about as unorthodox as it could be, but the main thing is that he always displayed the greatest courage, and he will be remembered as one of the finest sportsmen who ever donned a running shoe.[2]

According to folklore, Liddell ran that 400 metres Olympic final clutching a piece of paper that was pressed into his hand on the start-line. On it was written, 'Them that honour me I will honour 1 Samuel 2:30.' Whether this is an apocryphal story or not, Liddell's devotion to his faith superseded all else. He left Scotland, where he had grown up as the son of a Church of Scotland minister, to become a missionary in China. He died of a brain tumour in a Japanese internment camp in February 1945. He was 43 years old.

To mark the seventy-fifth anniversary of Liddell's gold medal in Paris, Donald Walker wrote in The Scotsman in the summer of 1999,

The 100 metres title did go to a Scotsman eventually. Allan Wells was asked after winning the blue riband of the 1980 Games if he would dedicate his 100 metres gold medal to Harold Abrahams. 'No; replied Wells, 'this one was for Eric Liddell.'

The grave where Liddell rests in China was unmarked until 1991, when it was located by ex-pat Charles Walker, and a slab of Mull granite was shipped out as a memorial befitting a national hero. 'Everyone has a different view of Liddell,' said Walker. 'Some see him as an athlete, some as a Christian, some as simply a fine human being: This weekend, we should see him as all those things, and as a true sporting hero.[3]

Edwards admits that at the time of his refusal to participate in the Olympic trials he was not consciously following the example of Liddell. 'I was vaguely familiar with his name, but I didn't draw any parallels. When others chose to write about me in company with Liddell it was obviously flattering, an honour to be thought of alongside him. But I think the biggest challenge to being likened to Eric Liddell is having to live up to what he achieved beyond the athletics arena. He committed himself to serve God and, though he could have used success by staying in Scotland and sharing the gospel, he bravely went as a missionary to China. He was an exceptional man. He won Olympic gold, but we remember him as a man of faith. It would be something if the same could happen to me!

Unlike Liddell, Edwards was naturally targeted by the media. There was a rush to interview him from the moment his objection to competing on a Sunday became known. 'I was really a nobody, yet there was this incredible media attention. I wasn't prepared for that! Nor was Val Davison, at the time head of department in the cytogenetics laboratory where Edwards was working. Her department came under siege.

Television crews and a posse of reporters and photographers were dispatched to the Royal Victoria Infirmary to try to get Edwards' story. There were more newsmen attempting to dial into the hospital. Davison recalls, We ended up blocking the telephone calls. It's a very sensitive type of work that we do and I was unimpressed to have all the lines tied up. Frankly, the last thing you want in a

---

2 *World Sports*, June 1948.
3 *The Scotsman*, 10 July 1999.

genetics department is a lot of media attention for whatever reason!

Edwards could not grasp the scale of the interest. 'It was unbelievable! I had piles of messages saying phone, phone, phone, phone, phone! On the day of the trials, television crews turned up outside his church, the Heaton Baptist Church, with the ambition of filming him going in to worship. Unfortunately for them, Edwards had kept a pre-arranged appointment and gone away for the weekend.

The next day the media was still on his trail. Would the selectors award the third, discretionary place on the team to Edwards? Eventually, he took a call at the laboratory from a member of the British team management, telling him he had been selected for Seoul. 'I can remember being ecstatic and jumping up and down. I was going to the Olympics...'

Davison, now the director of the regional genetics laboratory at Birmingham Women's Hospital, shared his joy that afternoon in Newcastle. She had been a loyal supporter of Edwards from the day when, against all odds, she had appointed the youthful-looking Physics graduate to her department on an initial six-month contract. We were delighted; everyone in the lab wanted to help Jonathan because he's so genuine, such a lovely person: remembers Davison, who in the early summer of 1999 had just returned from trekking in the Himalayas. We were quite a small group and all of us were athletic, in our own pathetic little way. We all did things like the Great North Run, gentle sort of running, and we all went to the gym at lunchtime. We were a fairly fit group, so I think to have somebody there who had the potential to be a real athlete was quite exciting for us. I remember at the time having an argument that went on and or with our personnel department over trying to get Jonathan leave on full pay for the Olympics. I think he had to have a period of about six weeks off. Personnel said fine, he can have the time, but we're not going to pay him. It was an ongoing argument. I think we won, if not totally, then almost, and that was an achievement'

Those Olympics were never destined to offer Edwards anything other than experience, but the concept of competing on a Sunday was to remain anathema for him for another four years. He missed the Europa Cup when it was held at Gateshead on a Sunday in 1989, and he declined to jump at the World Championships in Tokyo in 1991.

He was now ranked No 1 in Britain. 'I've had lot of encouragement from the public: Edwards said at the time. The decision not to compete was very much between my conscience and God. What I do in sport comes out of my dedication to God. The coverage I've had through not competing on a Sunday has been immense. That's given me a chance to share with people how important my faith is. God has used it, I'm sure, to give me a chance to tell people what a difference being a Christian has meant to me. Even though it upsets me to miss out on competition I'm being true to the thing that's the most important part of my life. It will get harder as it goes on. If I come to 1992 and the Olympics beckon and the event's on a Sunday, that will be hard. But I would accept it because that's what has been decreed.'

In their parish of Bearwood in Bournemouth (they had moved from Ilfracombe in 1989), Reverend Andy Edwards and his wife Jill were quietly proud of their son. 'One of the tragedies of our environment today is that a principled stance has become rare: said Reverend Edwards. 'Unless you go with what everyone else does, you're a stick-in-the-mud; funny. Obviously, from a practical view there was some disappointment because there was an increasing number of competitions on a Sunday. Here's a person who has ability, a gift God has given him and he is unable to use it and that seems a frustration. But there is a principle and Jonathan felt if he honoured God, then God would honour him.'

Imagine, then, Edwards' relief and gratitude when the schedule for the Barcelona Olympics was published. The qualifying rounds for the triple jump were to be held on Saturday 1 August 1992, the final on Monday 3 August. 'A miracle, divine intervention,' he smiled. As it transpired, Edwards had a wretched Games in Barcelona, failing to make the final, and it caused him to reassess his relationship with God. Seven weeks later, however, he finished the year with a courageous victory in the World Cup in Havana, Cuba, despite being ill.

It was through the ensuing winter months that Edwards was to arrive at a momentous crossroads. Every major triple jump competition in 1993 was to be staged on a Sunday. Edwards was stunned. He still looked as if he could have been a fresher at Durham University, but he was 26 years old and in control of his own destiny. He took a far-reaching decision. At the beginning of 1993, he told the world that from now on he would compete on a Sunday.

In the summer of 1999, Reverend Edwards sits in the lounge of his vicarage in Cumbria and admits, 'At times, if I'm really pushed, I wonder how completely right it is what Jonathan has done: For Jill Edwards, her son's decision was a huge surprise too. 'Initially, I was disappointed, but it did make me go back to the drawing board says Jill.

She read the Bible with new purpose, seeking explanations.

There was also genuine anxiety on their part that their
son might have erased all the good work he had done. They
feared that he might now be held in scornful contempt,
dismissed as just another guy on the make. 'I think we were
worried that Jonathan would completely spoil the good
witness that he has of being a truthful man', adds his
mother. 'We never stopped respecting or loving him in any
way, though, and we knew that he wouldn't have made any
decisions lightly'.

Edwards knew that his change of heart would distress
his parents, but he could not allow this to influence him.
He was now intending to be accountable for his own
actions. His own wife, Alison, had counselled him hard
before he opted to go public with his radical U-turn. 'I was
terrified mainly because of what other people would think
and the effect it would have on his Christian witness; she
says. 'But this was Jonathan's stand; he was the one who
didn't jump on a Sunday. I remember saying to him he had
to be sure what he was doing'.

Alison confirms that her husband's parents found the
decision difficult to accept. For Edwards this would have
been especially hard, given how exceptionally close he has
been to his mother throughout his life. He would have
hated to cause her any pain. 'It was something Jonathan
prayed through and it was very difficult for his Mum and
Dad, probably the one real major difference they have had.
They didn't agree he was doing the right thing, but this was
Jonathan making his own stand. This was him saying, "This
is what's right for us." We made the decision, gently told
people and battened down the hatches waiting for this
barrage of criticism – "How could you?" or "You

hypocrite!" – but, by and large, nothing came and we were grateful for that.'

During the time that Edwards was changing his mind, dismantling a once strongly held principle, his brother Tim was on a six-month devotional stay at a Bible School near Lancaster in the company of his wife Anna. Tim wrote to his brother, posing a set of penetrative questions. 'Although there was no way that he could be a fully professional athlete and not jump on a Sunday, I wanted to know: Does that make it right? Could he still be a Christian athlete and make that stand? Was what he was doing wise? I thought I'd ask the questions that perhaps hadn't been asked. That was my thinking when I wrote, not that I didn't agree with him' Jonathan would admit years later, 'When I got a letter from Tim, I realized this had to be a really serious issue because we're both notoriously bad at corresponding.'

Like Jonathan, Tim had been brought up by his parents to acknowledge that Sunday was to be preserved for worship and the family. Tim, however, has since taken his wife and three young daughters with him to Israel, where he will complete his Masters in Jewish Civilization at the Hebrew University in the year 2000. 'I work on Sundays now; he explains. 'The church I attend meets on a Sunday because that's when the English-speaking services are held and Anna doesn't speak Hebrew. After church, I'm straight to the university. I don't work on Friday evening to Saturday evening as no one else does. It's the Sabbath and the libraries are closed.' So for Tim Edwards and his family the board has moved, just as it has for his brother and his family.

In the summer of 1999, shortly after hearing the lingering worries of his parents, Edwards ventures, 'At some point towards the end of 1992, I came to the realization that it was not wrong to jump on a Sunday. Then the issue of course became: Was it wrong for me? Having made such a public stand, people would accuse me of convenient compromise. A bit of success, and I could hear people thinking, "Okay, here we go, another guy chasing the dollar." People could suppose it was easy for me to turn my back on jumping when I wasn't anybody, but now I'd started to jump reasonably well, my athletics was going to take over.

'I was very, very worried because that was not the case. But there's a verse in Proverbs 29 which spoke very directly to me about my circumstance. It states, "Fear of man will prove to be a snare" (v. 25). I think what that means is simply that being worried about what other people think of you can compromise your commitment to God. I'd gone into athletics to serve God. That had been very recently challenged with the whole Barcelona experience and I felt I'd come through to a closer walk with God and a stronger, more deep-rooted desire to serve him. I felt I could make the decision with integrity within the context of my Christian faith and the fact that I'm doing athletics to serve God.'

Also at around this time, Edwards received a visit from a friend who felt compelled to tell him of a dream in which he had featured. Extraordinarily, Richard Taylor's dream seemed to confirm Edwards' interpretation of the quotation from Proverbs 29. Taylor, a fellow member of the congregation at Heaton Baptist Church, had seen his friend standing on the edge of a runway on an athletics track. Edwards was waiting to jump, but could not because the runway was blocked by a host of people. Taylor came and cleared the crowd. Edwards says, 'After the people had gone, I was able to run and jump … and I jumped miles.

That was Richard's dream, so vivid that he felt he had a responsibility to tell me.'

The two men had not discussed Edwards' reconsidered feelings to competing on a Sunday, but the athlete made a near-instant connection. 'I think this was the fear of man as a snare, the fear of other people's reactions that was stopping me from doing what I believed was the right thing to do. You read often in the Bible about God speaking directly; I do believe that God spoke directly to me there. I think this was because it was such a big decision, potentially the worst decision I could ever have to make. The press could have been forever cynical about Jonathan Edwards, which rightly or wrongly would have coloured the whole of the nation's impression of me.

Edwards chose the quarterly *Christians in Sport* magazine in which to publish his decision. Unbeknown to Edwards, the director of coaching for British athletics at the time, Frank Dick, also sent a letter to be published in the same issue of *Christians in Sport*. Dick wrote,

> I'm writing comment because, without knowing what he will write, I do know that he will be unwilling to state just how hard it was for him to balance all the factors involved and make the decision he did. You will, I hope, have gathered that I am talking about Jonathan Edwards, the young man who overcame food poisoning to win the triple jump in this year's Athletics World Cup in Cuba. He's a very special person. He'd fight to the death for his team-mates, the flag he proudly wears on his vest, and for his deeply held beliefs. He fought even harder in reaching this decision. I'm very proud to know him. He is a most outstanding ambassador for his sport, for his country – and most important of all – for his beliefs and the values he holds highest.[4]

---

4 *Christians in Sport* magazine, March 1993.

Alison Edwards' assertion that her husband escaped all criticism is not quite true. Colin Hart from the *Sun* newspaper recalls, 'We were at the World Indoors Athletics Championships in Toronto and I remember Jonathan sitting down with a group of writers and he came out with a story that God had spoken to him in a dream and told him that now it was quite all right for him to jump on a Sunday. And, of course, being the old cynic that I am, I thought, "Oh yeah, it's suddenly dawned on this young man that most of the major events are going to be on Sundays. And if he doesn't jump on a Sunday he's never going to make it as an international athlete, nor is he going to make any money at his business. When he first made his decision not to jump on a Sunday the sport was not as professional, there wasn't the money to be won. What a wonderful way to get round the problem, through a dream someone else had." Whether we were cynical or not, however, he was obviously a nice young man and you couldn't get away from that fact. He was so genuine, he believed it, so because of who he was there wasn't a great song and dance made of it.'

Surprisingly, the most barbed attack on Edwards' re-evaluation is delivered by Norman Anderson, a close friend of the family as well as his weightlifting coach. In advance of my meeting with him, Anderson told Edwards that if he spoke, he would want to speak from the heart. To his credit, Edwards told him he would want him to do just that, and so we hear Anderson, unabridged and raw. 'It's a complete myth to compare Jonathan with Eric Liddell,' he says. 'There is no comparison. He wouldn't compete on a Sunday, Liddell, and he stuck to it. Jonathan decided that perhaps he could.'

Anderson is registered blind and over 60 years old, but

he is regularly lifting weights in the gym at Gateshead Stadium as he still competes in power-lifting in his age group. Before he began working seriously with Edwards in 1995, Anderson was part of a group who lifted in the gym at times when the athlete was present – men like Peter Gordon and Arthur McKenzie, both international discus throwers in their prime, and Bob Morton, who owns a gym they sometimes used. There was a lot of good-natured humour, as they tried to persuade Edwards to jump on a Sunday.

Ironically, once he had established in his own mind that he would be no less a Christian for jumping on a Sunday, Edwards' decision was met with a wave of cynicism within that same band of men, according to Anderson. 'The cynical view was, "Hallelujah, one of Jonathan's friends has had a dream, so now it's all right to jump on a Sunday," ' says Anderson. 'How convenient, when you knew you had to jump on a Sunday if you were going to make any money.'

Yet perversely, Anderson insists he does not wish to sound critical. 'I think Jonathan has made the right decision; he says. 'I think he's absolutely right. He's a talented man and he has made a good living. If he had been my son, I would have told him to get out there, for goodness' sake. So I'm not criticizing I'm just saying how his decision is seen by some of those around here.'

Edwards' decision was bound to stir emotions in those closest to him. His coach at that time was Carl Johnson, who had been with him since he arrived in the Northeast to attend Durham University. Now Johnson says solemnly, 'His decision to compete on a Sunday perturbed me greatly; it perturbed me greatly because I felt it was wrong for him to make what was a decision that altered the principle of his life. I didn't want him to regret it 10 years down the line, and I'm still not sure about it.

'It was necessary from the point of view of his athletic development because he was being denied opportunities in major competitions. His development was being slowed down. Now once he opened that up, he was able to develop as an athlete, but that's not the be-all and end-all, you see. It's to become a right and comfortable person, to be eventually comfortable with yourself. What worried me at that time was, all right, he was comfortable, he could rationalize, explain it, but what happens in 10 years? What's he going to think at the moment he comes to die? None of us know this, do we? But is that not where your actions in this life are really quite important?'

Edwards has continued through the years to receive letters from Christians expressing both disappointment and encouragement over his change of heart. With the passing of those years, he has also come to articulate better how he arrived at the point where he felt able to compete on a Sunday. On 30 October 1999, he offered his thoughts for publication in this book.

The editing of this chapter, reliving some of the events surrounding 'Sunday' and my athletic career, has been a sobering experience. I have had to smile as well as wince at some of my comments and, indeed, those of my biographer: 'He was 26 years old and in control of his own destiny ...' At 33, I probably feel less in control of my destiny than I ever did.

What still amazes me is that not-jumping-on-a-Sunday is an image that endures seven years on. You're that athlete who doesn't jump on a Sunday; said the man who came to fix our oven recently. 'A real Christian, you are; not like the rest of them who are only in it for the money: He spoke in a manner that did not invite response, so I smiled and mumbled a 'thank you' and let the conversation pass to another subject.

Unknowingly, that gentleman had hit on the heart of the issue; an issue that this book has brought to my attention again. Because I do now jump on a Sunday. Because I am still a 'real Christian' ... or am I?

The one major fault I now see in the manner in which I handled the announcement of my 'Sunday' decision was that I never gave a clear biblical basis for it. If this foundation does not exist, then I am very much open to the criticism of not being the genuine article.

I initially wrote a much longer, more detailed article that outlined what I see as the biblical justification for my change of heart, and this now appears in an appendix at the end of the book. I hope that this briefer, less technical piece will serve as a more accessible insight into my thought processes, as well as providing a reassurance of my continued commitment to serve God with my whole heart.

The crux of the matter, I believe, hinges around the application of the Old Testament Law to New Testament believers. The Law that God gave to Israel after her deliverance from Egypt, the Law that contains the Sabbath commandment, delineated the way he wanted the Hebrew nation to live their lives. The question is this: Does God call those who follow him today to live by the same set of commands?

The Bible is not a theology textbook; it is not a book we can just casually pick from the shelf, choose a random passage and apply it directly to our lives. Some thought is needed. To whom was the passage originally addressed? What were the unique historical circumstances? How does this relate to other portions of the Bible? This is not to assert that God can only speak to us through certain parts of Scripture, but only to say that care is needed when we try to understand and apply God's written Word.

These considerations come to bear directly on the Sunday debate. The Old Testament is clear: 'Remember the Sabbath day by keeping it holy' (Exodus 20:8). The New Testament seems ambivalent: 'One man considers one day more sacred than another; another man considers every day alike. Each one should be fully convinced in his own mind' (Romans 14:5). Which one is right?

Well, both are; they just apply to different groups of people living at different points in history. The first command, from the Old Testament, is part of the Law given to Israel and the second, from the writings of the Apostle Paul, is directed to the church in Rome. But what about us, believers living in the third millennium?

As Christians today, we are part of the Church, the world-wide group of followers of Jesus Christ, and we share a direct and vital continuity with those believers whom Paul was addressing. Therefore, it would be my belief that it is the latter command, the New Testament imperative, that is applicable.

It was this conclusion that I reached at the end of 1992: as a present-day believer, it was not wrong for me to jump on a Sunday. I cannot emphasize strongly enough that I would never have made the decision if I did not have this belief. The verse from Proverbs and the dream played their part in helping me overcome the fear of making a U-turn, but its foundation rested firmly on God's Word.

So when the man who repaired the oven noted that I was a real Christian, one who would not compromise his beliefs for personal gain, I hope he was mistakenly right!

Reverend Andy Edwards and his wife Jill had not read this piece prior to their own review of their son's decision. 'Jonathan will always give an honest answer about his trust in God,' says his mother. 'Quite clearly, people who write about him and interview him realize that. His integrity has never been questioned.' Reverend Edwards admits, We had to look at ourselves and discover why we felt like we did, think about what we believed. There was also a duty to see it from Jonathan's perspective. I understand what he does and I value what he does. If he's going to be the witness that he wants to be as a Christian in the athletic world, he's got to be where they are. I totally understand that and fully endorse that.'

His parents, of course, were both in Seville in August 1999 to support Edwards' fruitless attempt to regain the World Championship title. The depth of their commitment to their son cannot be overestimated.

Edwards himself places great importance on the fellowship he now receives from the friends he has made at Holy Trinity Church, dose to his home in the Newcastle suburb of Gosforth. He still attends church on most Sundays and when he is at home he is a devotee of the midweek fellowship meetings that are held on Wednesdays. Spiritually, he was feeling strong in the autumn of 1999.

He smiles, too, at the recollection of the first competition he entered on a Sunday. 'It was the European Cup in Rome and on my first jump I was given a white flag. But the television replay showed that it was a clear foul – you could even see the mark in the plasticine. If I had been struck by a bolt of lightning, one might perhaps have drawn the conclusion that God wasn't too happy with me! Instead, I got a gift'

Edwards is drawing a humorous line in the sand, of course, but the reality is this: the issue is closed. He can stand on the track on any day of the week with a clear conscience.

The God Catchers

Tommy Tenney

Have you ever wondered why it sometimes feels as if God is hiding from you? Tommy Tenney certainly experienced such feelings. They launched him on a journey of discovery to encounter God more intimately.

'Now I am no longer content just to "chase" Him, I want to "catch" Him'.

'God doesn't hide Himself from you,' says Tommy, 'so that He can't be found; He is very careful to hide so that He can be found… We will never leave his presence unchanged.'

Bestselling author of The God Chasers, pastor and well-known revivalist, Tommy shares with us his passion for the presence of God.

Thomas Nelson, Inc (Word)
ISBN: 0-7852-6653-4

Price: £8.99

£6.99 with money off voucher

Chapter 1

Does God Play Hide-And-Seek?

Things I Wish I Knew The Day I
Nearly Caught Him

Have you ever wondered why it sometimes feels as if God is hiding from you? I know I've felt that way sometimes. Perhaps that is why He launched me on a journey of His own choosing when He interrupted my self-defined successful career as a full-time evangelist with a simple but shocking revelation: *You know, Tommy, your favorite services and My favorite services are not the same. You leave your services full and satisfied, but when you leave, I'm still hungry.*

God whispered this to me during a life-changing early Sunday morning service. It was a divine encounter that forever imprinted itself with indelible ink on the pages of my memory. In a way, I could almost identify with how Isaiah felt the day he suddenly saw God "high and lifted up" in the temple long ago.[1]

There were tears in my eyes when I whispered to my wife, "I don't think I've ever been this close to Him before." Hundreds of other people who were in the building that day will testify to the same sensation. It is as if we "caught" Him.

I wish I knew then what I have discerned since – that God will leave our meetings full and satisfied only when we begin to leave them feeling hungrier for Him than when we first came.

The Lord began to teach me about the importance of being a *God Chaser* during a nine-month period of what I call "divine discontent." It culminated in an encounter with Him – an encounter from which I have never recovered.

Now I am no longer content just to "chase" Him. I want to "catch" Him, to collect a string of close encounters with Him. Sometimes I grow weary with the daily chase, but I must chase if I want to catch.

During that period of growing discontent, God planted in my heart the seeds for a book titled *The God Chasers.* I had no idea that book would ignite such a firestorm of hunger for God. I knew only how hungry I was.

My desire to sustain the collected moments with God made me feel the frustration of Jacob: "If I ever get my hands on Him, I'll not let go." And there is where I discovered another piece to the puzzle of His presence – and the message for this book – only this time it came while I was hiding behind a closet door.

God used my youngest daughter to teach me about Himself once again. Class began with the sound of her little bare feet padding across the linoleum floor and the sight of her irresistible smile as she said, "Let's play hidey-face, Daddy!"

I'm sure you played similar games with your children. I played hidey-face with all my girls. My most recent play partner was my youngest daughter, so my memories of her joyful discoveries during the hidey-face game are the freshest.

My memories began when she still wore those over-sized plastic-coated disposable diapers that made a telltale *whoosh-whoosh* sound every time she walked. I tracked her every step as she looked for me in all the strange places that seem so logical from a toddler's point of view. I listened from my hiding place behind the closet door as she looked for me in the oven, in the trash bin, and in the ridiculously crowded space under the kitchen sink.

With growing anticipation I listened to my little pursuer's every move because I had a plan in mind. Every minute seemed like an hour for me because I was waiting for the joy of our encounter. I could barely wait to see her face light up the moment she discovered her long-lost daddy.

If it was clear that my petite pursuer was having trouble finding me, then I would be careful to leave something showing to help her along. If I was behind the closet door, then I'd make sure part of my foot was showing. If I took refuge behind the couch, then I'd make sure that just enough of my backside showed to help her find me.

Why be so careful? It is simple: the point of our elaborate game of hidey-face wasn't the hiding; it *was the finding!* I wasn't hiding from my little girl so that she couldn't find me; I was careful to hide so that she *could* find me.

Then I remembered that God did the same thing with Moses. If you recall, He was careful to leave part of His divine "backside" showing so Moses could see Him. Evidently Moses was a lot like my daughter because he wasn't satisfied with that. He wanted more. He wanted to see God's face; he longed to see His glory.

We Come to Church for Different Reasons Than God Does

I've continued to learn more about the pursuit of His presence since I first started chasing Him. I wish I had known these things the day I "almost caught Him."

I've learned more about the fuel of desperation and the feel of destiny while in pursuit of His presence. The Lord also taught me more about embracing the place of what I previously called a "frustrating funk, a divine depression of destiny"[2] Weariness with man can birth desperation for God.

Even then I had hints in my heart that, in some supernatural way, the pursuer becomes the pursued when God catches wind of our worship and praise. I was beginning to understand the power of collective hunger where corporate visitations of God were concerned.

Isaiah's vision of God in the sixth chapter of his prophetic book occupied a prominent place in my early understanding of the way God revealed His manifest presence to men. The Holy Spirit has opened my eyes to see this same scripture passage from a totally new viewpoint – one that has everything to do with catching God, so to speak.

I didn't realize it at the time, but I was speaking prophetically of this book when I wrote about that encounter with God's manifest presence in *The God Chasers:*

> The instant Isaiah the prophet, the chosen servant of God, saw the King of glory what he used to think was clean and holy now looked like filthy rags. He was thinking, *I thought I knew God, but I didn't know **this much** of God!* That Sunday we seemed to come so close; we almost caught Him. Now I know it's possible.[3]

If you can get that close, you can catch Him! Often, when we wander off in the wrong direction in our pursuit of Him, God calls out to us to help us along. When my youngest daughter and I played hidey-face, I loved to hear the lyrical sounds of her "little girl giggle" just bubbling with excitement. I loved it so much that if she wandered off in the wrong direction and stopped giggling in her search, then I would call out and say, "Over here ... closer ..."

Then I would listen to her stop and *be still* while she tried to locate the source of Daddy's voice. *I am convinced that God does the same thing.*

One day a young man named Samuel was searching for Him, and evidently he got really close to where God was hiding. When he failed to find Him, God whispered, "Samuel ..."

Then God's young pursuer promptly went running in the wrong direction as we often do! In our immaturity, we often chase after man's voice thinking it is God's voice. Only repeated attempts by God and truth from ministers can help us locate the source of that "still small voice."

God keeps trying. Perhaps now it is time for the ministry to say, "It's not *us* ... even if you hear Him through our voices ... it's not us." Respond to Him! Speak to Him!

"Eli, was that you?"

"No, that wasn't me."

"Samuel ..."

What was about to happen? *A God Chaser was about to become a God Catcher.* Even elderly Eli had "cornered" God a few times. He said, "Samuel, let me tell you how to respond the next time you hear that voice." Then he taught Samuel the simple but profound process by which you capture God in that moment of divine encounter.

Why would the God of the universe, the almighty

Creator, hide Himself from His creation? We know, for instance, that He hides Himself from sin and pride, basically because He doesn't want His absolute holiness to destroy us in our pollution. But that isn't the main reason that God hides. He sent His only Son to take care of the sin problem forever once we repent and turn to Him. I think the biblical answer has more to do with joy than with judgment.

I often tell the story of the years when my youngest daughter was still riding a big yellow bus to school each day. She's reached that "grown up little girl stage" now where she doesn't like to ride buses anymore because "they're hot and sweaty," but I miss the joyful encounters I had with her when that bus rolled up to our driveway.

At the end of a long ministry trip, I began to miss her and her older sisters so much that I'd skip sleep and take an early flight just so I could beat them home from school.

Some of the greatest highlights in my memories are those afternoons when I could sneak home early so I could be standing in the driveway when the school bus pulled up.

I love to pass through the treasured mental snapshots of my girls growing up, and some of the best close-ups I remember come from those precious moments of joyful reunion in the driveway.

The pursuit and "capture" of God is a process. When my youngest daughter stepped off that yellow school bus, she went through a very similar process with me. I can still see it in my mind. She stepped off the bus surrounded by all her little buddies, talking a mile a minute, with her sweater dragging on the ground and one shoe untied. (That's why sweaters last only one year – when little kids get off the school bus, they drag them along behind with their backpacks.)

I lived for the moment her eyes found me. Suddenly she forgot everything around her except for one thing: "Daddy! Daddy! Daddy!" After three short steps, the sweater was on the ground, followed by the backpack three steps later. Then I had to brace myself because I knew she was going to launch herself at me in a desperate lunge of love.

The scene that captures my mind is the look of sheer excitement on her face. I had surprised her, and she was overjoyed. She knew I was coming home, but I met her early when she least expected it.

She was immersed in the liquid joy of discovery and delighted by the unexpected excitement and serendipitous moment of encounter, *"It's him!"* Then we enjoyed about thirty seconds of sheer pleasure as we went through our private process of rediscovery and delight.

First she would jump in my arms. After a crushing hug I had to swing her around and around in a circle with her feet flying in the air while she laughed and giggled uncontrollably. When I finally set her down, she wanted to kiss me again.

At that point, I would usually turn away "Why?" you may ask. "Didn't you want to be kissed?" Of course, I did, but I knew that if I turned away, it would make my little girl pursue me even harder and she would give me even more kisses. It was a very well-organized plot. *I didn't run away* – I turned away.

The moment I turned away from my little girl, she would get "the look" on her face and start the process again by saying with all the determination she could muster: "I'm going to kiss you, Daddy!"

"No, you're not kissing me. Look at you. You are all dirty! You've got mud all over you – you're not kissing me!"

"I'm going to kiss you, Daddy! I'm going to kiss you."

"No, you're not kissing me."

And so the game began again. She was determined to kiss me, but it wasn't hard for me to avoid her. I could easily move my two-hundred-and-none-of-your-business pounds this way and that way to dodge her.

Within a few minutes, she would get tired and say, "Oh, Daddy," and stop her pursuit. She couldn't capture me physically, but she easily captured me emotionally. She couldn't move her legs fast enough to apprehend me, but her words easily captured my heart.

Some people take offense at my use of the term *God Chaser,* saying, "You don't have to chase God." I understand but I don't agree. You may call it whatever you want; it doesn't bother me. My youngest daughter didn't have to chase me to get me to be her daddy, but if she wanted more than just to live in the same house, if she wanted attention and affection, then she knew which "buttons" to push. You may be content just to be in God's house, but I want to be in His lap!

I do agree that none of us can ever really catch Him. That much is obvious. His ways are as far removed from our ways as the east is from the west. None of us can catch Him through physical effort, mental gymnastics, or passionless spiritual exertion. "Works" can't catch Him, but an appeal to mercy and grace … !

The "catching" will come if you can ever get to that point of weary desperation where you just say, "Oh, Daddy!" All of a sudden, you capture and enrapture the heart of the God you can't take captive any other way The One you are chasing will suddenly become the One who pursues you!

If You Are a Worshiper, God Will Track You Down!

At the very moment my little daughter would say, "Oh, Daddy," I would turn and begin to chase her. Worship turns the tables on the chase. It takes you to the point where you don't have to pursue Him because He begins to pursue you. If you are a worshiper, God will track you down. He will find you even if you are left in the bottom of a Philippian prison with your hands in chains as Paul and Silas were. If you are a worshiper, He will track you down and seek you out.

It is as if He stands up in heaven and says:

"I smell worship."
"Where is it coming from, God?"
"I don't know, but I'm going to find it right now"

Worship and spiritual hunger make you so attractive to God that your circumstances cease to matter anymore. He will move heaven and earth to find a worshiper. When you begin to worship with all your being and desire, your heart turns Him toward you. You capture His attention and attract His affection.

It transforms you from being a God Chaser to the potential of being a God Catcher. Your worship essentially sets a "lover's entrapment" for Him. If the Song of Solomon is any indication, then this kind of "passionate entrapment" is His delight.

Let me return to the simple illustration of a father playing with his children. It is nearly impossible to get my adolescent daughters to play hidey-face with me anymore. When they were newborns, all I had to do was smile, and they would gurgle with excitement. Then I moved up to the more advanced game of hiding my eyes with my hand. I could keep them laughing, cooing, and gurgling almost endlessly with that simple act of hiding and finding again.

Ultimately they moved to greater independence when they began to walk and our game involved more separation and much more seeking, but it still ended in a riotous reunion marked by the joy of fresh encounter. My three daughters have nearly outgrown the game of hidey-face now, so I have to seek out the two-year-old children of my assistants because they are still at that age of joyful discovery.

It is normal for children to grow up, but God defines another kind of normal for His kingdom. The only way to understand what I'm talking about is to become like a little child. I think I read that somewhere too. Did you read the same Book? "Unless you are converted and become as little children, you will by no means enter the kingdom of heaven."[5]

As I said, when my children were little, I would often hide from them. Yet the hiding wasn't the purpose of the whole game. The joy of finding and being found was the purpose of the game. *The hiding was just something I had to do to create the moment that I wanted.*

I thought nothing of waking up at four o'clock in the morning after ministering in a long evening service and enduring six to eight hours in airports and on the plane just so I could experience thirty seconds of my daughter's joy in the driveway. Of course, five minutes later she was ready to play with the kids in the neighborhood. Even so, it was worth it for me to be there to see her. That was the whole purpose. *It was worth it.* God will take a trip in time just to spend a brief moment with humanity. He thinks it's worth it to be with you!

God loves it when you discover Him, but how can you discover Him if He doesn't sometimes hide? The Scriptures are full of examples showing that God "hides." The Bible records, "Seek My face," and "Seek the LORD while He may be found."[6] The most important thing I've learned, and the most important point in this book, is this:

He hides for the sheer joy of being discovered.

Even though my youngest daughter has partially outgrown the hidey-face game, I can still manage to squeeze some great kisses and hugs from her if I really work at it. The other day I said, "Honey, come up here and give Daddy some love. Give me some kisses."

She was busy playing with some of her dolls and things, but she obediently crawled up on my lap and gave me a kiss. Then she was ready to get down again.

"No, come on. Give me some more love," I said.

Then she said, "That's the problem with you daddies."

"What do you mean?" I said.

"You always want too much love," she said.

I could only grin and say, "Yeah, I'm guilty."

That's the problem with our Daddy too: *He always wants too much love.* We give Him a perfunctory kiss on Sunday morning and hurry to return to our religious toys and pretend encounters. All the while He is saying, "I've been missing you; I'd love to have some more loving kisses and hugs from you."

God loves it when we want to linger in His presence, but those times are rare in most modern churches. We've become more time sensitive than Spirit sensitive. Whatever happened to "waiting on God"?

This book has one simple and straightforward focus:

how you can capture God's heart. It's not that you must run faster to catch God, because you can never run fast enough to overtake Him. However, if you pursue His heart in passionate hunger, your words of desperation have the power to capture and "corner" His heart. In that moment, the Pursued becomes the Pursuer and the God Chaser becomes the God Catcher.

As a father, I am constantly conniving to squeeze just one more hug or kiss from the daughters I love so much. I suspect our heavenly Father does the same. Our problem in the church is that if we are not careful, the arrogance of our spiritual adolescence robs us of our childlike passion for His presence. More than anything else, we must learn that *God does not hide so that He* cannot *be found; He is very careful to hide so that He* can *be found.*

Notes

1 See Isaiah 6:1.
2 Tommy Tenney, *The God Chasers* (Shippensburg, PA: Destiny Image Publishers, 1998), p. 2.
3 Ibid., p. 10.
4 See Psalms 10:1; 13:1; 27:9; 44:24; 55:1; 69:17; 88:14; 89:46; 102:2; 104:29; 143:7.
5 Matthew 18:3.
6 Psalm 27:8; Isaiah 55:6.

Faithworks

Steve Chalke

Political leaders are talking about the real need for greater involvement by voluntary groups – including churches, Christian charities and other faith–based agencies – providing welfare care.

They're beginning to recognise what Christians have known all along. From homelessness to health care, job clubs to children's clubs…faith works! But churches often find themselves discriminated against purely on grounds of religious conviction.

Faithworks sets out to gain recognition for the contribution of local Christian groups, acknowledge the role that faith plays and encourage and promote government funded initiatives.

Steve Chalke is an author, TV and radio presenter, international speaker and founder of the Oasis Trust.

Kingsway Publications
ISBN: 0-85476-966-8

Price: £4.99

£3.99 with money off voucher

Published by Kingsway Publications
Lottbridge Drove, Eastbourne, BN23 6NT, England

Chapter 1

Seize the Day

'There are three things I don't like about you.' The then head of the Council Housing Department wasn't a man to mince his words. I'd just outlined our plan to set up a small, referred-access hostel for homeless young people in his borough, and he was somewhat underwhelmed by our proposal, to say the least.

'First,' he explained, sneering at me as I sat in his office, 'you're a Christian. Second you're an *Evangelical* Christian.' After these two I wondered what would come next. 'Third,' he announced, 'you're a minister. We don't need any hostels run by your type around here. If you open, it'll be over my dead body!'

I don't know what happened to him, but we did open. It took over four years to turn our vision into a reality, but we managed it. And Oasis, the charity I started over 15 years ago with the specific aim of opening that one hostel, now runs a range of different facilities for homeless people in London's inner city.

And our approach works: figures from that first hostel show that around 80 per cent of the young people who've stayed there and then been 'resettled' by us have held down a job and stayed in housing for at least three years after leaving us. They're making a contribution to the community around them rather than remaining the 'victims' of society.

What's more, in spite of the vehement protests of that Head of Housing over a decade ago, the local council is now in absolutely no doubt just how good a job we do. A senior representative of that same London borough council admitted to me recently that our resettlement figures were impressive – in fact, they were ones he wished other hostels on his patch could emulate.

Yet amazingly we still find ourselves constantly facing religious discrimination. Sometimes the element of faith gets deliberately left out of the equation, shunted carefully out of the limelight like an embarrassing relative. Many of our projects have been praised by local statutory bodies, but always in terms that take no account whatsoever of the tact that we're a faith-based charity. Just as often, however, we've found that our faith has positively counted against us. All of our homeless facilities struggle to find enough money to meet their modest running costs, for example, and yet bureaucracy has blocked statutory funding to us time and again simply because we're a specifically Christian agency.

And we're far from alone. Faith-based agencies of all kinds, especially Christian ones, tend to find themselves being effectively discriminated against purely on the grounds of their religious convictions. For a whole host of reasons – from the groundless suspicion that all Christian care is really just a covert attempt at church 'recruitment' to straightforward anti-Christian prejudice – a great many churches and Christian charities find themselves constantly having to 'hide their light under a bushel' in their dealings with local statutory bodies. In effect, they're forced to choose between either massively downplaying their religious core and commitment or missing out on taking a vital stake in local community action. They risk losing both opportunities for partnership and vital funds and resources from local authorities.

We've never engaged in any underhanded attempts at proselytism, nor have we in any way foisted our beliefs on our residents or clients – though, by the same token, we've never tried to conceal them. But to our staff of committed Christians, faith has always been a very powerful source of both motivation and inspiration. If you asked any of them why they were prepared to work long hours for comparatively little pay, and why their job gave them such enjoyment, their faith would come at the very top of their list of reasons.

> On the threshold of a century of opportunity, ours is a society with no more vision of where it is going than those stumbling home early on New Year's Day. The Dome is a fitting national symbol, a wonderful structure that stands for nothing, a stunning shell with a hole where the heart should be.
>
> The Times, 1st January 2000

Why, then, should one of the key things that makes us so effective, and has helped us establish such a good track record as a care provider, be an embarrassment or an impediment when it comes to getting recognition, respect and vital resources? Why are local councils, and some other governmental organizations, still suspicious of the role that our faith plays in our work? Why should we have to de-emphasize our Christian ethos and vision when it's such an integral part of who we are?

Faith works

The truth is, it's faith that drives churches and Christian
charities up and down the UK to get involved in care and
welfare provision in the first place. It's faith that pushes us
to develop a clearer understanding of the massively complex problems at issue within society, and to strive for more
effective medium- and long-term solutions. It's faith that
motivates us to keep going when the going gets tough and
the mission ahead looks impossible.

In short, it's faith that compels us, in the famous words
of St Francis of Assisi, to work to 'sow love where there
is hatred, pardon where there is injury, faith where there
is doubt, hope where there is despair, light where there is
darkness, and joy where there is sadness'.

Social reform is about far more than resources and
externals. Real change comes from within. The greatest
poverty our nation faces is a poverty of hope. That's why
Christian faith is potent. Faith transforms lives, and that's
why faith *works*.

Faith isn't just a key motivator for people to get involved
in projects linked to welfare provision; it's also a key motivator for them to stay involved in these projects. What's
more, it helps to ensure that their involvement is the kind
that produces genuine long-term creative outcomes: positive, professional, practical, personal and persevering.

Faith-based agencies, by their very nature as faith-based
agencies, are watermarked by five characteristics that are
essential components in any meaningful, realistic approach
to care and welfare provision. The care they offer is:

Rooted

Faith-based agencies, especially churches, aren't just local, they're also firmly rooted to specific geographical communities. They're a permanent part of those communities, 24 hours a day and 365 days a year. They don't clock off at 5 p.m. – they're there for the long haul. And that means they not only come face to face with all the problems and needs of their community, day after day, but they also have to live with the reality of all those problems and needs themselves – not to mention the consequences of the various approaches taken to solve them! Churches and other faith-based groups therefore have a real depth of insight into their local community, and a vested interest in improving its welfare on both the pastoral and practical fronts.

Sustainable

Because they're locally rooted, churches and other faith based groups necessarily take a long-term view of the problems and needs of their area. They know that the 'quick fix' approach doesn't work. All too often they've seen the disastrous results of the 'here today gone tomorrow' attitude taken by too many organizations in the past,

including local or perhaps even national governments more worried about elections than real results, as well as various well-meaning but badly informed quangos (quasi autonomous non-governmental organizations). In most cases, 'quick fix' solutions have created more harm than good. As a result, local churches are striving for real, work able medium- and long-term solutions.

Committed

One of the key differences between an effective charity organization and an ineffective one is the motivation levels of its staff and volunteers. The sheer scale and complexity of the issues faced by most voluntary sector groups offering care and welfare is totally daunting. Tackling the same, seemingly insurmountable, problems day after day can seem about as worthwhile and sensible as trying to turn back the tide. The advances and achievements that do happen seem so tiny by comparison with the task still to be done. To keep going in the face of wave after wave of what can frequently appear to be nothing more than constant setback and futility requires deep reserves of energy and vision – reserves that are an integral part of faith.

Imaginative

One of the major side effects of having high levels of commitment and a real faith in the future, however, is a constant determination to find new ways around or over obstacles. *Stupidity is doing what you did yesterday again today and expecting a different result.* Faith breeds a can-do culture, and a can-do culture refuses to see any obstacle as final. For Christians, not even death is the end of the story.

God, not injustice or 'impossibility', has the last word. As a result, faith-based groups such as local churches approach problems with both optimism and imagination. They're not naïve – most are all too aware of their limitations but they are committed to being as flexible and imaginative as possible, determined not to give up until they've found a way round a problem, or removed it entirely. Our commitment to constantly seeking innovative ways forward springs from our understanding of the principle of incarnation, – the very core of our faith. God became one of us. He inventively accommodated himself to our culture in order to meet our needs.

Transforming

Poverty isn't just a material problem; it's a spiritual one as well. Personal, internal change is an essential ingredient in real social transformation. Throwing money at social deprivation can only ever provide temporary solutions to the problems confronting our society. That's why Christian faith is so potent it develops the strength and health of both individuals and communities. Put simply, faith sparks transformation. Churches, aware that every individual is made in the image of God and personally loved by him, are highly motivated to give them the individual time, respect and dignity that no administrative system can ever offer. People begin to believe in themselves when they know that someone else believes in them. And when people begin to grasp their own importance and value as individuals, not only are they transformed, but they also help to transform others. The wheels of genuine social transformation begin to turn.

> In Britain, the Judaeo–Christian foundation to our society has played a key role in fashioning the social concern that becomes the welfare state. But we are mistaken if we think we can subcontract the social concern and compassion demanded by our faith to the state and simply leave it there. There is a growing recognition that the state can do many things well, but it cannot deliver the personal or spiritual support that we all need to overcome life's greatest adversities.
>
> Gary Streeter, MP

Actions speak louder than words

We now stand at the threshold of an enormous opportunity.

In the run-up to the General Election, the major political parties are beginning to sing from the same song sheet. They're talking about the need for greater involvement by different voluntary groups, including churches and Christian charities, in providing welfare to those on the margins of society.

In July 2000, both Prime Minister Tony Blair and Conservative leader William Hague took time out of their schedules to address 'Faith in the Future', the millennium conference of the UK's black majority churches. Both men praised the vital role that black churches have played in rejuvenating not just black culture, but British culture as a whole. What's more, they recognized the role that black majority churches, and other churches, will play in the future in the areas of education, employment and community development.

Blair spoke of how black majority churches have been active in 'enriching' and 're-energizing' society. He welcomed the interest many black churches had shown in setting up 'City Academies' – state-funded, independently run secondary schools. 'Faith communities have an important part to play in this,' he told delegates. Hague was just as strong. 'There is plenty of evidence that inner-city children who are involved with their local church have a much greater chance of escaping poverty and drug addiction. The work that churches have been doing on strengthening families, teaching parenting skills, and micro-employment projects gives us a clear idea of the way we should go,' he remarked. 'Your churches stand as shining lights of hope in communities which feel disadvantaged and discriminated against.'

There is, however, still a massive gap between the rhetoric and the reality. At present, there are no clear policies or concrete proposals to ensure these good intentions are matched in practice.

The truth of this was hammered home to me after a very positive meeting with staff in Downing Street about the possibility of setting up a City Academy. The supportive attitude of Westminster's corridors of power seemed to evaporate the moment we crossed the river and started dealing with the London borough in which we actually planned to run the school. The language of support gave way to the language of suspicion. In marked contrast to the warm and enthusiastic response we'd received from the different parliamentary political parties, the local council saw our Christian faith and foundation as a real problem.

It is to bridge this gap between rhetoric and reality that Oasis has launched *Faithworks* – not just this book, but a whole *Faithworks Campaign* aimed at putting in place concrete structures on the ground to ensure that faith-based groups (Christian and otherwise) aren't allowed to be the continued victims of religious discrimination when it comes to welfare provision initiatives. We're not asking for favoured status, just a level playing field. From home-less-ness to health care, from job clubs to children's clubs, from back-up for young parents to care for elderly grand-parents – local churches and Christian charities throughout the UK demonstrate seven days a week, 365 days a year, that *faith works*. But in borough after borough, council after council, quango after quango, we find ourselves being discriminated against simply because of the role played by our faith.

Faith is good, not bad. It's progressive, not regressive. It's empowering, not enslaving. Our faith is a genuine asset, not a liability, when it comes to providing best quality, cost-effective care. Faith is the engine that drives the church's work. So our message to government is: *Don't remove our engine!* Don't let other people's prejudice force us to behave as if our faith isn't a vital, life-giving part of who and what we are. For us at least, no faith, no works. Let our records speak for themselves. Rather than hampering our efforts by forcing us to downplay the importance of our faith, help us by recognizing that it's a major key to our success. It lies at the heart of our motivation and effectiveness as care providers. Don't rob us of this essential ingredient. Don't make us act like agnostics to gain your confidence or respect.

That's why our message to our political leaders and representatives – whoever wins the next General Election – is simple: you talk a great game, but we've yet to see this translated into reality. It's time to put your muscle (and your money) where your mouth is.

Fresh Power

Jim Cymbala

Jim Cymbala cuts through the theological clutter about the Holy Spirit with this fundamental truth: We need the Spirit desperately.

All our cleverness can't transform a single addict, or bring a jaded businessman to Christ. Only God's Spirit can do that.

Drawing from examples from the Bible and from the sidewalks of New York City, he shows what happens when the Spirit of God moves in our midst.

'Fresh Power' will expand your vision and inspire you to pray for the power of the Spirit in your church and in you.

Jim Cymbala has been pastor of The Brooklyn Tabernacle for more than twenty-five years.

Zondervan Publishing House
ISBN: 0-310-23685-5

Price: £8.99

£6.99 with money off voucher

PROLOGUE

by D.L. Moody

Toward the end of the nineteenth century, the greatest Christian evangelist alive at that time called a special convocation. D. L. Moody summoned people to his hometown of Northfield, Massachusetts, "for prayer and waiting upon the Lord for a new enduement of power from on high." Moody, who had started out his working life in the shoe business, had never received ordination but nevertheless was greatly used of God both in America and across Great Britain, seeing hundreds of thousands come to Christ. He became a household name among believers everywhere. He was known and appreciated as a careful student of the Bible, staying humble amid his great popularity.

But Mr Moody's heart became increasingly concerned over the years as he saw spiritual decline in so many churches. How could he, as an evangelist, effectively extend God's kingdom if the local congregations were lukewarm? Where would converts go to be fed and nurtured?

In response to Moody's appeal, hundreds came from nearly every state and several foreign countries for the meetings conducted during this special convocation. His talks were condensed into a book published a few months later under the title Secret Power.[1] It began as follows:

There has been much inquiry of late on the Holy Spirit. In this and other lands, thousands of persons have been giving attention to the study of this grand theme. I hope it will lead us all to pray for a greater manifestation of His power upon the whole church of God.

How much we have dishonored Him in the past! How ignorant of His grace and love and presence we have been! True, we have heard of Him and read of Him, but we have had little intelligent knowledge of His attributes, His offices, and His relations to us....

Let others reject, if they will, at their own peril, this imperishable truth. I believe, and am growing more into this belief, that divine, miraculous, creative power resides in the Holy Spirit....

Unless He attend the word in power, vain will be the attempt in preaching it. Human eloquence or persuasiveness of speech are the mere trappings of the dead. If the living Spirit be absent, the prophet may preach to the bones in the valley, but it must be the breath from heaven that will cause the slain to live....

If we want that power to quicken our friends who are dead in sin, we must look to God, and not be looking to man to do it. If we look alone to ministers, if we look alone to Christ's disciples to do this work, we shall be disappointed. If we look to the Spirit of God and expect it to

---

[1]   Dwight L. Moody, *Secret Power* (Chicago: Moody, 1881).

come from Him and Him alone, then we shall honor the Spirit, and the Spirit will do His work.

I cannot help but believe that there are many Christians who want to be more efficient in the Lord's service. It is from the Holy Spirit that we may expect this power.

Chapter 3

Something from Heaven

Imagine that by some time-warp technology you could zoom back two thousand years to the upper room in Jerusalem a week after the ascension of our Lord. As you stand there in a corner, I want you to take a close look at the men and women sitting in this place. Scan the crowd and look into their faces. What do you see? Think about who they are and where they come from.

The first obvious question would be about the apostles and why the Lord Jesus chose these particular men as leaders. Why didn't he select rabbis and scholars of the Law? He could have chosen gifted orators who could sway thousands with their powers of speech. Instead, you see fishermen. You see a former tax collector. You see a former member of the Zealots, a radical political group. You see ordinary men. No executive search process would ever have selected them for such crucial leadership. These are the last people you would pick to launch a religious movement.

Of course, Jesus did this on purpose. He knew it would be almost impossible for them to depend on their human ability; instead, they would have to reach out to his promise of "power from on high." He recognized that all too often the more educated people become, and the brighter they are, and the better their connections to human influence, money, and power ... the more they tend to look away from the power of God. They trust in God's grace less and less.

Even worse than what I have already described is that this upper-room group included men of recent spiritual failure. Just a few weeks ago, at a moment of crisis, they deserted their leader. Their three-year discipleship experience under the teaching of Jesus suddenly went out the window. All the lessons they had learned (and who could have taught truth more perfectly and brilliantly than the Son of God?) seemed to count for nothing. They had watched his example in every kind of circumstance; they had seen him stand up to pressure in the midst of vigorous debate with the Pharisees; they had held their breath as he courageously cast out the powers of darkness. Yet, when their own hour of crisis came, they bailed out. When push came to shove, they ran for the shadows. All the good teaching and good example evaporated into the nighttime chill of Gethsemane.

And not only did they show a surprising cowardice, but one of them, Peter, lurched into a full-blown denial of Jesus. In fact, three times he said he didn't even know Christ – the last time punctuated with profanity.

A couple of days later, when Thomas was told that Christ had come back from the dead, he was so steeped in doubt and self-pity that he replied, in essence, "No way! That's impossible."

Would you want to build any kind of a future on this group? I wouldn't.

A forlorn lot

Yet there these men sit in the upper room, simply waiting, praying, perhaps singing at times. A deep sense of aloneness claws at their spirits. Memories of Jesus flit across the inner screen of their minds ... the time Jesus walked on the water, the time he stilled the storm, the times he fed huge crowds. Now all that is in the distant past, and Jesus is far away somewhere ... they don't really know where.

They are tormented by reminders of how they failed their Master in his neediest hour. Maybe they should just go outside and disperse. But that could be dangerous, couldn't it? They are, after all, in the middle of Jerusalem, the city that just cried out for Jesus to be crucified and certainly has no love for his former followers. What will become of them after all?

Yes, he had said as he left them that they would receive some kind of *power* when the Holy Spirit came upon them (whatever that might mean) and would be his witnesses to the ends of the earth. But how could that happen? Who was this other Counselor who would be with them forever and make them into mighty men of God? Surely some unimaginable, powerful someone or something would have to change them into spiritual champions.

And then the Scripture tells us:

> When the day of Pentecost came, they were all together in one place. Suddenly a sound like the blowing of a violent wind came from heaven and filled the whole house where they were sitting. They saw what seemed to be tongues of fire that separated and came to rest on each of them. All of them were filled with the Holy Spirit and began to speak in other tongues as the Spirit enabled them (Acts 2:1–4).

I am not so much concerned to focus on the individual phenomena here – the wind, the fire, the speaking in tongues – as I am to hold up the main truth that *something supernatural came from heaven and invaded men and women on earth, changing them forever.*

I think we have lost the wonder of that because we are so familiar with the passage. Since the Holy Spirit *is* God, what is the depth of meaning in those words "all of them *were filled with the Holy Spirit*"? They were filled with God himself!

Forget for a moment what you have been taught by others about this phrase. Open yourself to what God did here. Frail men and women were not just given help around the edges, but were filled with God the Holy Spirit.

Power for the Present

Who can deny that this is the great need in our churches today? This is what all pastors desperately require, starting with me. We need something with the mark of heaven upon it. Too much of our religious life is made up of pro-grams and human ideas, talents and strategies. While these have value, they pitifully fail to meet the need of the hour. What is missing today is something from heaven itself, something from God the Holy Spirit that fills and floods our lives.

This has always been God's design for his church. Take, for example, the Bible's statement "If anyone speaks, he should do it as one speaking the very words of God" (1 Peter 4:11). How long has it been since you heard that kind of authoritative, heart-searching preaching? Instead, too many church meetings have become increasingly predictable and dull. Many enemies of Christianity over the centuries have become confirmed in their agnostic opinions by going to churches that purported to be "Christian" but were dreadfully barren and spiritually dead. How could God be real and powerful if this kind of church was his major advertisement? Never mind just quoting verses from the Bible; they were looking for some sign of Christianity working itself out through real flesh and blood.

Many people today, even church members, agree with the critics, although they're too polite to say so. Everything in the service may be doctrinally sound – but there's nothing *from heaven* that grips them. Too often we are found discussing only words and phrases, doctrinal positions and denominational traditions – but where is the power of the Holy Spirit in all of this?

By contrast, we see the New Testament church and its ministers regularly having encounters with the living God. This sense of the divine brought hardened sinners to their knees. The powerful word stabbed their consciences. The Holy Spirit produced a climate that was anything but dull and ordinary.

And in fact, this kind of anointed preaching evoked controversy. The upstanding citizens of at least one city, Thessalonica, moaned, "These men who have caused trouble all over the world have now come here" (Acts 17:6). It is sadly the same in our churches today. The very mention of God's promise of "something from heaven" makes people nervous if it seems that the boat might get rocked or if there might be a departure from the order of service printed in the church bulletin.

But have you ever been in a meeting where, let's say, a song touched your heart in a probing yet tender way? It wasn't just a combination of lyrics and notes; it was a message made alive to you by the Holy Spirit. Have you ever sat listening to a sermon that stirred your heart to its depths and spoke powerfully to your own spiritual need? You sat there saying to yourself, *There's no way this speaker could know what I'm like or how I'm struggling right now. And yet this message is like he 's been reading my mail. God must have told him what to say today.*

Wind, Fire, Voice

What God did on the Day of Pentecost was dramatic and powerful. One of the biblical symbols of the Holy Spirit is wind, and the wind in the upper room that day wasn't just a little breeze; it was "violent," according to Acts 2:2. In many of us, we need just such a strong wind to blow out the rubbish that has accumulated. Many of our churches need a typhoonlike visitation of the Spirit of God. We need a major renovation of our spiritual lives, not just a rearrangement of the furniture. Think how whole cities and towns would be affected if Christian churches began praying for the wind of God to blow upon them.

Fire is another Holy Spirit symbol, and tongues of fire formed that day over each of the 120 heads in the room – men and women alike. It wasn't the apostles alone. God the Holy Spirit visited each believer, since all of them needed his power equally to accomplish God's will for their individual lives.

After that, the people in the upper room spoke in languages they did not know except as "the Spirit enabled them" (v. 4). The ecstatic tongues that flowed from these ordinary people were identified by visitors from all around the Mediterranean who had come to Jerusalem that week. The immediate result of their baptism with the Holy Spirit was that they began to do something they could not normally do.

Without getting into the debates that have arisen about speaking in tongues, let us focus on the main point of this passage: God by his Spirit enabled ordinary men and women to do and say things beyond their natural abilities. They became supernaturally empowered. There was no human explanation for what was taking place.

This is the story, in one way or another, of every man, woman, or church that has ever been used in great ways for God's glory. They were set on fire by God, and that experience affected the world around them.

Praise God for his ability to lift us above ourselves! Otherwise, where would all of us be? Especially people such as my wife, Carol, and me, who never got to go to a Bible college or seminary ... others who say, "I don't have this talent or that ability." We can take courage from the fact that these fishermen and others – "losers" by the world's standards – were invaded by God and raised to amazing places. The same tongues that had engaged in petty argument about who was the greatest, the same tongues that had denied the Lord and the fact of his resurrection were now overtaken by heaven itself and put to use "declaring the wonders of God" (v. 11).

The Holy Spirit is still greater today than all our shortcomings and failures. He has come to free us from the restraints and complexes of insufficient talent, intelligence, or upbringing. He intends to do through us what only he can do. The issue is not our ability but rather our availability to the person of the Holy Spirit.

In fact, this is God's ordained way of equipping us, because it leaves little doubt about who should get all the glory. If our human intellect and abilities and talents produced the results, we could strut around saying, "My, we're pretty special, don't you think?" (By the way, that is the very attitude of too many churches that are run on the basis of programs and human talent rather than the manifest power of the Holy Spirit.)

But men and women who are truly used by God are necessarily humbled, because they know the true source of their strength. Think of how Peter and the others rejoiced that night as they fell asleep in their beds. God's grace and the power of the Spirit had proven greater than their human failure and limitations.

Jesus told the disciples one time, "When they arrest you, do not worry about what to say or how to say it. At that time you will be given what to say, for it will not be you speaking, but the Spirit of your Father speaking through you" (Matthew 10:19–20). We see this happening time and again in the book of Acts, not only for Peter and Paul but for others such as Stephen: They are hauled into court, and from their lips comes suddenly a message with the mark of the Holy Spirit upon it.

I am not against sermon notes and outlines for ministers. But isn't it tragic that many pastors often spend hours polishing every nuance of their sermons while hardly investing much time at all in prayer and waiting upon God to be freshly filled with the One who can supernaturally assist them? What we need today is not cleverness or oratory – we need messages from God's Word set on fire by the Holy Spirit!

D. L. Moody, as you may know, never had the formal credentials to be ordained. That is why he was always called simply "Mr. Moody." He was short, stocky, and not particularly attractive in appearance. He mispronounced words regularly. If you read his personal letters, you will see all kinds of punctuation and spelling errors.

Yet he addressed more people and brought more of them to Christ than anyone else in the nineteenth century. How did that happen?

Well, Moody said that the turning point was something that happened just across the East River from the borough of Brooklyn, where our church is located – while he was walking on Wall Street no less! In late 1871, just a few weeks after the great Chicago fire, the thirty-four-year-old Moody had come east to try to raise money to rebuild the buildings he had lost. But, he writes,

> My heart was not in the work of begging. I could not appeal. I was crying all the time that God would fill me with His Spirit. Well, one day, in the city of New York – oh, what a day! – I cannot describe it. I seldom refer to it; it is almost too sacred an experience to name…. I can only say that God revealed Himself to me, and I had such an experience of His love that I had to ask Him to stay His hand. I went to preaching again. The sermons were not different; I did not present any new truths, and yet hundreds were converted. I would not now be placed back where I was before that blessed experience if you should give me all the world.[1]

Oh, that all of us might receive, like Mr. Moody, something fresh from the Holy Spirit that revolutionizes our spiritual lives!

---

[1] Cited in V. Raymond Edman, *They Found the Secret* (Grand Rapids: Zondervan, 1960), pp. 83–84.

A curious crowd

The coming. of the Spirit upon the disciples and his divine enablement brought a large crowd together, the first such audience that showed any interest in the followers of the recently crucified Jesus. Crowds will always gather when the Holy Spirit is working in the midst of God's people. Peter recognized the evangelistic opportunity and stood up to preach. How would he do?

This was a man who had little, if any, formal education and was by trade a fisherman. This was the one who less than two months before had vociferously renounced the Lord. This was the man who, even after seeing the resurrected Lord, opted to forget the ministry and go back to fishing (John 21). This was the man who in sensitive situations was infamous for putting his foot in his mouth. What respectable church today would let this man into its pulpit! Can you hear the introduction, "Congregation, let's give a warm welcome today to Brother Peter, who just a few months ago denied he even knew Jesus...."? I doubt it.

In fact, Peter spoke marvelously with clarity and power. He quoted both the prophet Joel and the book of Psalms at length, apparently from memory. When he finished, the crowd was "cut to the heart" and began to call out, "What shall we do?" (v. 37). By the end of the meeting, some three thousand people had been saved. Not a bad first outing for the rookie preacher.

What made the difference? The only variable in the equation was that now Peter had been taken over by the Holy Spirit. It is staggering to remember that Peter walked with Jesus for three years and received teaching, discipleship, and a moral example unparalleled in all of history. And yet all of that never made Peter the man God intended him to be. It is not until we see Peter "filled with the Holy Spirit" that things really turned around. No wonder Jesus excitedly assured them that greater days were coming for all of them when the Holy Spirit, their invisible Helper, came upon them in power.

As Samuel Chadwick succinctly put it, "The Christian religion is hopeless without the Holy Ghost."[2]

To that I would add, ministry is especially hopeless without the Holy Spirit. Let every pastor take note: Our attempt at ministry will be an absolute exercise in futility if we are not expecting and experiencing divine help through the power of the Holy Spirit.

It is not enough to teach and preach about the Spirit. We must experience him personally in new depths, or we will accomplish little. Without the Holy Spirit there is no quickening of the Scripture. Worship is hollow. Preaching is mechanical, never piercing the heart. Conviction of sin is almost nonexistent. Faith is more mental than heartfelt. Prayer meetings fade away. Church meetings become routine. And Christian people stay lukewarm at best.

Please, God, send the Holy Spirit upon us and revive your people.

I am not issuing any kind of call for fanaticism. We don't need musicians working up the audience into some kind of frenzy. We don't need manipulated manifestations or counterfeit gifts. But we do need the real Holy Spirit upon us in power, in all our churches, of all denominations and traditions.

Listen to Chadwick's bold indictment from a century ago:

---

[2]   Samuel Chadwick, *The Way to Pentecost* (reprint, Dixon, MO: Rare Christian Books, n.d.), p. 11.

The church still has a theology of the Holy Spirit, but it has no living consciousness of his presence and power. Theology without experience is like faith without works: it is dead. The signs of death abound. Prayer meetings have died out because men did not believe in the Holy Ghost. The liberty of prophesying has gone because men believe in investigation and not in inspiration. There is a dearth of conversions because faith about the new birth as a creative act of the Holy Ghost has lost its grip on intellect and heart. The experience of the second gift of grace is no longer preached and testified because Christian experience, though it may have to begin in the Spirit, must be perfected in the wisdom of the flesh and the culture of the schools. Confusion and impotence are the inevitable results when the wisdom and resources of the world are substituted for the presence and power of the Spirit.[3]

What Christian here in the new millennium cannot agree that we desperately need a fresh filling of the Holy Spirit? Isn't that the heart-cry of Scripture, even long before the book of Acts? The prophet Isaiah pleaded with God,

Oh, that you would rend the heavens and come down,
    that the mountains would tremble before you!
As when fire sets twigs ablaze
    and causes water to boil,
come down to make your name known to your enemies
    and cause the nations to quake before you!
For when you did awesome things that we did not
    expect,
    you came down, and the mountains trembled before
    you.

3   Chadwick, *The Way to Pentecost*, p. 13.

Since ancient times no one has heard,
>   no ear has perceived,
no eye has seen any God besides you,
>   who acts on behalf of those who wait for him
>   (Isaiah 64:1–4).

How long has it been in many of our churches since God "did awesome things that we did not expect"? Maybe it is because we have not done what the last line suggests, in waiting before God as they did in the upper room. The Christian life, like the life of Jesus on earth, is a combination of waiting and activity, of prayer and service. Jesus spent time alone with the Father in solitary places and then went forth in power to face incredibly busy days of ministry to needy people. Likewise, we must balance all our activities *for* him with time spent *with* him, waiting in expectant prayer and worship. We must avoid the idea that well-intentioned Christian service and doing things for God will ever amount to much without fresh infillings of the Spirit's power.

Admittedly, we must also beware of the opposite: a pseudo spiritual life of spending time alone with God without ever getting out among the people and laboring with all our strength to bring them the gospel. Consider the proper biblical balance of human effort and dependence upon the Spirit's power: "To this end *I labour,* struggling with all *his energy,* which so powerfully works *in me*" (Colossians 1:29). Would to God that more of us ministers could honestly say this verse about our own lives.

Cry of the Heart

What stops us today from drawing a line in the sand and setting our hearts toward God in fervent prayer that he will come and revive his work in us as well as in our churches? Soon our lives will be over, and it is better to live a few years full of the Spirit, seeing God work in and through us, than to go on for decades with little or no experience of the great things God has promised to his people through the person and work of the Spirit.

In a world as tormented and confused as ours, we desperately need God's wind and fire to energize us. With sin on the rampage and demonic powers controlling more and more of our culture, we need an enduement of divine power similar to what God gave the early church. Why don't we stop rationalizing and justifying the spiritual impotence all around us? Why not rather humble ourselves and seek God with all our heart for "something from heaven"?

The Mark

Tim LaHaye and Jerry B. Jenkins

The gripping apocalyptic drama continues with Book 8 The Mark in the most successful Christian fiction series ever – Left Behind.

Forty-two months into the Tribulation, the gloves are off and the battle is launched between the forces of good and evil.

With over 34 million copies sold around the world, Left Behind, a fictionalised interpretation of the book of Revelation, has prompted many – Christians and non believers – to consider what might happen after the Rapture.

Dr Tim LaHaye, who conceived the series, is a renowned prophecy scholar. Jerry B. Jenkins, the writer, is the author of more than one hundred books.

Tyndale House Publishers, Inc.
ISBN: 0–842–33225–1
(hardback)

Price: £15.99

£12.99 with money off voucher

One

It was mid afternoon in New Babylon, and David Hassid was frantic. Annie was nowhere in sight and he had heard nothing from her, yet he could barely turn his eyes from the gigantic screens in the palace courtyard. The image of the indefatigable Nicolae Carpathia, freshly risen from three days dead, filled the screen and crackled with energy. David believed if he was within reach of the man he could be electrocuted by some demonic charge.

With the disappearance of his love fighting for his attention, David found himself drawn past the jumbo monitors and the guards and the crowds to the edge of the bier that had just hours before displayed the quite dead body of the king of the world.

Should David be able to see evidence that the man was now indwelt by Satan himself? The body, the hair, the complexion, the look were the same. But an intensity, an air of restlessness and alertness, flowed from the eyes. Though he smiled and talked softly, it was as if Nicolae could barely contain the monster within. Controlled fury, violence delayed, revenge in abeyance played at the muscles in his neck and shoulders. David half expected him to burst from his suit and then from his very skin, exposed to the world as the repulsive serpent he was.

David's attention was diverted briefly by someone next to Carpathia, and when he glanced back at the still ruggedly handsome face, he was not prepared to have caught the eye of the enemy of his soul. Nicolae knew him, of course, but the look, though it contained recognition, did not carry the usual acceptance and encouragement David was used to. That very welcoming gaze had always unnerved him, yet he preferred it over this. For this was a transparent gaze that seemed to pass through David, which nearly moved him to step forward and confess his treachery and that of every comrade in the Tribulation Force.

David reminded himself that not even Satan himself was omniscient, yet he found it difficult to accept that these eyes were not those of one who knew his every secret. He wanted to run but he dared not, and he was grateful when Nicolae turned back to the task at hand: his role as the object of the world's worship.

David hurried back to his post, but someone had appropriated his golf cart, and he found himself peeved to where he wanted to pull rank. He flipped open his phone, had trouble finding his voice, but finally barked at the motor-pool supervisor, "I had better have a vehicle delivered within 120 seconds or someone is going to find his —"

"An electric cart, sir?" the man said, his accent making David guess he was an Aussie.

"Of course!"

"They're scarce here, Director, but —"

"They must be, because someone absconded with mine!"

"But I was going to say that I would be happy to lend you mine, under the circumstances."

"The circumstances?"

"The resurrection, of course! Tell you the truth, Director Hassid, I'd love to get in line myself."

"Just bring —"

"You think I could do that, sir? I mean if I were in uniform? I know they've turned away civilians not inside the courtyard, and they're none too happy, but as an employee —"

"I don't know! I need a cart and I need it now!"

"Would you drive me to the venue before you go wherever it is you have to g —"

"Yes! Now hurry!"

"Are you thrilled or what, Director?"

"What?"

The man spoke slowly, condescendingly. "A-bout-the-res-ur-rec-tion!"

"Are you in your vehicle?" David demanded.

"Yes, sir."

"That's what I'm thrilled about."

The man was still talking when David hung up on him and called crowd control. "I'm looking for Annie Christopher," he said.

"Sector?"

"Five-three."

"Sector 53 has been cleared, Director. She may have been reassigned or relieved."

"If she were reassigned, you'd have it, no?"

"Checking."

The motor-pool chief appeared in his cart, beaming. David boarded, phone still to his ear. "Gonna see god," the man said.

"Yeah," David said. "Just a minute."

"Can you believe it? He's got to be god. Who else can he be? Saw it with my own two eyes, well, on TV anyway.

Raised from the dead. I saw him dead, I know that. If I see him in person, there'll be no doubt now, will there? Eh?"

David nodded, sticking a finger in his free ear.

"I say no doubt, eh?"

"No doubt!" David shouted. "Now give me a minute!"

"Where we goin', sport?"

David craned his neck to look at the man, incredulous that he was still speaking.

"I say, where we going? Am I dropping you or you dropping me?"

"I'm dropping you! Go where you want and get out!"

"Sorry!"

This wasn't how David normally treated people, even ignorant ones. But he had to hear whether Annie had been reassigned, and where. "Nothing," the crowd-control dispatcher on the phone told him.

"Relieved then?" he said, relieved himself. "Likely. Nothing in our system on her." David thought of calling Medical Services but scolded himself for overreacting.

Motor-pool man deftly picked his way through the massive, dispersing crowd. At least most were dispersing. They looked shocked. Some were angry. They had waited hours to see the body, and now that Carpathia had arisen, they were not going to be able to see him, all because of where they happened to be in the throng.

"This is as close as I hope to get in this thing then," the man said, skidding to a stop so abruptly that David had to catch himself. "You'll bring it back round then, eh, sir?"

"Of course," David said, trying to gather himself to at least thank the man. As he slid into the driver's seat he said, "Been back to Australia since the reorganizing?"

The man furrowed his brow and pointed at David, as if to reprimand him. "Man of your station ought to be able to tell the difference between an Aussie and a New Zealander."

"My mistake," David said. "Thanks for the wheels." As he pulled away the man shouted, "Course we're all proud citizens of the United Pacific States now anyway!"

David tried to avoid eye contact with the many disgruntled mourners turned celebrants who tried to flag him, not for rides but for information. At times he was forced to brake to keep from running someone down, and the request was always the same. In one distinct accent or another, everyone wanted the same thing. "Any way we can still get in to see His Excellency?"

"Can't help you," David said. "Move along, please. Official business."

"Not fair! Wait all night and half the day in the blistering sun, and for what?"

But others danced in the streets, making up songs and chants about Carpathia, their new god. David glanced again at the monstrous monitors where Carpathia was shown briefly touching hands as the last several thousand were herded through. To David's left, guards fought to block hopefuls from sneaking into the courtyard. "Line's closed!" they shouted over and over.

On the screen, pilgrims swooned as they neared the bier, graced by Nicolae in his glory. Many crumbled from merely getting near him, waxing catatonic. Guards held them up to keep them moving, but when His Excellency himself spoke quietly to them and touched them, some passed out, deadweights in the guards' arms.

Over Nicolae's cooing —" Good to see you. Thank you for coming. Bless you. Bless you."— David heard Leon Fortunato. "Worship your king," he said soothingly. "Bow before his majesty. Worship the Lord Nicolae, your god."

Dissonance came from the guards stuck with the responsibility of moving the mass of quivering, jellied humanity, catching them as they collapsed in ecstasy. "Ridiculous!" they grumbled to each other, live mikes sending the cacophony of Fortunato, Carpathia, and the complainers to the ends of the PA system. "Keep moving. Come on now! There you go! Stand up! Move it along!"

David finally reached sector 53, which was, as he had been told, deserted. The crowd-control gates had toppled, and the giant number placard had been trampled. David sat there, forearms resting on the cart's steering wheel. He shoved his uniform cap back on his head and felt the sting of the sun's UV rays. His hands looked like lobsters, and he knew he'd pay for his hours in the sun. But he could not find shade again until he found Annie.

As crowds shuffled through and then around what had been her sector, David squinted at the ground, the asphalt shimmering. Besides the ice-cream and candy wrappers and drink cups that lay motionless in the windless heat was what appeared to be residue of medical supplies. He was about to step from the cart for a closer look when an elderly couple climbed aboard and asked to be driven to the airport shuttle area.

"This is not a people mover," he said absently, having enough presence to remove the keys before leaving the vehicle.

"How rude!" the woman said.

"Come on," the man said.

David marched to sector 53 and knelt, the heat sapping his energy. In the shadows of hundreds walking by, he examined the plastic empties of bandages, gauze, ointment, even tubing. Someone had been ministered to here. It didn't have to have been Annie. It could have been anyone.

Still, he had to know. He made his way back to the cart, every seat but his now full.

"Unless you need to go to Medical Services," he said, punching the number into his phone, "you're in the wrong cart."

In Chicago Rayford Steele found the Strong Building's ninth floor enough of a bonanza that he was able to push from his mind misgivings about Albie. The truth about his dark, little Middle Eastern friend would be tested soon enough. Albie was to ferry a fighter jet from Palwaukee to Kankakee, where Rayford would later pick him up in a Global Community helicopter.

Besides discovering a room full of the latest desktop and minicomputers – still in their original packaging – Rayford found a small private sleeping room adjacent to a massive executive office. It was outfitted like a luxurious hotel room, and he rushed from floor to floor to find the same next to at least four offices on every level.

"We have more amenities than we ever dreamed," he told the exhausted Tribulation Force. "Until we can blacken the windows, we'll have to get some of the beds into the corridors near the elevators where they can't be seen from the outside."

"I thought no one ever came near here," Chloe said, Kenny sleeping in her lap and Buck dozing with his head on her shoulder.

"Never know what satellite imaging shows," Rayford said. "We could be sleeping soundly while GC Security and Intelligence forces snap our pictures from the stratosphere."

"Let me get these two to bed somewhere," she said, "before I collapse."

"I've moved furniture in my day," Leah said, slowly rising. "Where are these beds and where do we put them?"

"I wish I could help," Chaim said through clenched teeth, his jaw still wired shut.

Rayford stopped him with a gesture. "If you're staying with us, sir, you answer to me. We need you and Buck as healthy as you can be."

"And I need you alert for study," Tsion said. "You made me cram for enough exams. Now you're in for the crash course of your life."

Rayford, Chloe, Leah, and Tsion spent half an hour moving beds up the elevator to makeshift quarters in an inner corridor on the twenty-fifth floor. By the time Rayford gingerly boarded the chopper balanced precariously on what served as the new roof of the tower, every one was asleep save Tsion. The rabbi seemed to gain a second wind, and Rayford wasn't sure why.

Rayford left the instrument panel lights off and, of course, the outside lights. He fired up the rotors but waited to lift off until his eyes had adjusted to the dark ness. The copter had but ten feet of clearance on each side. Little was trickier – especially to a fixed-wing expert like Rayford – than the shifting currents inside what amounted to a cavernous smokestack. Rayford had seen choppers crash in wide-open spaces after merely hovering too long in one place. Mac McCullum had tried to explain the physics of it, but Rayford had not listened closely enough to grasp it. Something about the rotors sucking up air from beneath the craft, leaving it no buoyancy. By the time the pilot realized he was dropping through dead air of his own making, he had destroyed the equipment and often killed all on board.

Rayford needed sleep as much as any of his charges, but he had to go get Albie. There was more to that too, of course. He could have called his friend and told him to lie low till the following evening. But Albie was new to the country and would have to fend for himself outside or bluff his way into a hotel. With Carpathia resurrected and the GC naturally on heightened alert, who knew how long he could pull off impersonating a GC officer?

Anyway, Rayford had to know whether Albie was "with him or agin him," as his father used to say. He had been thrilled to see the mark of the believer on Albie's forehead, but much of what the man had done in the predawn hours confused Rayford and made him wonder. A wily, streetwise man like Albie – one who had provided so much at high risk to himself – would be the worst kind of opponent. Rayford worried that he had unwittingly led the Tribulation Force into the lair of the enemy.

As the chopper rumbled through the shaft at the top of the tower, Rayford held his breath. He had carefully set the craft as close to the middle of the space as he could, allowing him to use 'one corner for his guide as he rose. If he kept the whirring blades equidistant from the walls in the one corner, he should be centered until free of the building.

How vulnerable and conspicuous could a man feel? He imagined David Hassid having miscalculated, trusting old information, not realizing that the GC itself knew Chicago was safe – not off-limits due to radiation. Rayford himself had overheard Carpathia say he had not used radiation on the city, at least initially. He wondered if the GC had planted such information just to lure in the insurgents and have them where they wanted them – in one place for easy dispatch.

With his helicopter free of the tower, Rayford still dared not engage the lights. He would stay low, hopefully

beneath radar. He wanted to be invisible to satellite sur-
veillance photography as well, but heat sensing had been
so refined that the dark whirlybird would glow orange on
a monitor.

A chill ran up his back as he let his imagination run. Was
he being followed by a half dozen craft just like his own?
He wouldn't hear or see them. They could have waited
nearby, even on the ground. How would he know?

Since when did he manufacture trouble? There was
enough real danger without concocting more.

Rayford set the instrument panel lights at their lowest
level and quickly saw he was off course. It was an easy fix, but
so much for trusting his brain, even in a ship like this. Mac
had once told him that piloting a helicopter was to flying a
747 as riding a bike was to driving a sport utility vehicle.
From that Rayford assumed that he would do more work by
the seat of his pants than by marrying himself to the instrument panel. But neither had he planned on flying blind over
a deserted megalopolis in wee-hour blackness. He had to get
to Kankakee, pick up Albie, and get back to the tower before
sunup. He had not a minute to spare. The last thing he
wanted was to be seen over a restricted area in broad daylight.
Detected in the dead of night was one thing. He would take
his chances, trust his instincts. But there would be no hiding
under the sun, and he would die before he would lead anyone to the new safe house.

In New Babylon frustrated supplicants had formed a new
line, several thousand long, outside the Global Community
Palace. GC guards traversed the length of it, telling people
that the resurrected potentate would have to leave the
courtyard when he had finished greeting those who happened to be in the right place at the right time.

David detoured from his route to Medical Services to hear the response of the crowd. They did not move, did not disperse. The guards, their bullhorned messages ignored, finally stopped to listen. David, looking puzzled, pulled up behind one of the jeeps, and a guard shrugged as if as dumbfounded as Director Hassid. The guard with the loudspeaker said, "Suit yourselves, but this is an exercise in futility."

"We have another idea!" shouted a man with a Hispanic accent.

"I'm listening," the guard said, as the crowd near him quieted.

"We will worship the statue!" he said, and hundreds in line cheered.

"What did he say? What did he say?" The question raced down the line in both directions.

"Did not Supreme Commander Fortunato say we should do that?" the man said.

"Where are you from, my friend?" the guard asked, admiration in his voice.

"Méjico!" the man shouted in his native tongue, and many with him exulted.

"You have the heart of the toreador!" the guard said. "Let me check on it!"

The news spread as the guard settled in his seat and talked into his phone. Suddenly he stood and gave the man a thumbs-up. "You have been cleared to worship the image of His Excellency, the risen potentate!"

The crowd cheered.

"In fact, your leaders consider it a capital idea!" The crowd sang and chanted, edging closer and closer to the courtyard.

"Please maintain order!" the guard urged. "It will be more than an hour before you will be allowed in. But you *will* get your wish!"

David shook his head as he executed a huge U-turn and headed to the courtyard. People along the way called out to him. "Is it true? May we at least worship the statue?"

David ignored most of them, but when clusters moved in front of his speeding cart, he was forced to brake before slipping around them. Occasionally he nodded, to their delight. They ran to get in a line that already stretched more than a quarter mile. Would this day ever end?

A New Chapter

Jill Gupta

For twenty-six years, Mick Whitburn led a life dominated by crime, drugs, and violence. His habitual response to anything or anybody was sarcastic, critical and cold. A former Hell's Angel and estranged from his family, he drifted from one encounter with the law to the next.

Now his life has been transformed by a faith in Jesus, though this did not happen overnight. He is still in and out of prison – but now it's as a volunteer leading Alpha groups and prayer meeting.

Today Mick works on the streets as a seller of the 'Big Issue' and preacher of the gospel.

OM Publishing
ISBN: 1-85078-373-X

Price: £5.99

£3.99 with money off voucher

First Published in 2001 by OM Publishing

OM Publishing is an imprint of Paternoster Publishing,
PO Box 300, Carlisle, Cumbria, CA3 0QS, UK

Chapter 9

A New Life

I'd had my own place for three weeks and was doing my usual trip to Victoria to pick up my copies of *The Big Issue* when I bumped into Geoff Hunter, who'd been in the hostel with Gavin and me. We went for a cup of tea and he told me he'd been given a bedsit in Pimlico, but he didn't need it because he'd moved in with his girlfriend in Chalk Farm. Geoff said I could rent the bedsit from him if I wanted and I jumped at the chance. Gavin was pleased because it meant he had somewhere to stay when he came into London, and I knew I was still welcome at his flat in Woolwich whenever I felt like a change.

I moved in at the end of the week and on the Monday took over Geoff's pitch at Victoria coach station, selling *The Big Issue* from 8 am to 10 am and then from 2 pm to 4 pm. Geoff put me in touch with people I could buy puff from and told me that his girlfriend, Kylie, could supply with me with hard drugs whenever I wanted them. She was getting drugs on prescription and sold them on the streets, so she knew just about every drug dealer around. Most evenings I went to her place or she and Geoff came to mine and we would drink a few ciders, smoke puff and

chat. It also became a habit for Kylie to give me a couple of
Valium to help me sleep.

Although the coach station was a good pitch, I also
travelled round to different parts of London selling the
magazine. I became quite familiar with the city streets and
learned where *The Big Issue* sold well and where it didn't.
One day, in the late summer, I found my way to Shepherd's
Bush. It was very hot and after two hours standing across
the road from the station I'd only managed to sell two
copies. I sat down on the pavement in disgust and put the
magazines in a heap beside me. I was thinking about where
I should go next, when an ice cream was thrust in front of
my face and a woman's voice said, 'I'm giving you this in
the name of Jesus.' I took the ice cream and stumbled to my
feet, but the woman was already half way down the road.

Some time after this incident, a traffic warden came over
to me and invited me to his church. He said one of the
church members would be able to help me find some
accommodation. I told him I already had somewhere to
stay. He moved on and I took up my pitch at the coach
station. I'd made up a little rhyme, '*Big Issue* 70p: if not, a
smile will do for me.' I repeated it every time a likely pur-
chaser walked towards me, and I was saying it when a
woman approached me and asked straight out, 'How do
you stand with God?' I gave an instant answer to this
strange and unexpected question. 'Not very good, I
suppose.' Then she asked me if I wanted to go to a nearby
café for a coffee and to say a prayer. I was all for a free cup of
coffee and there was no harm in saying a prayer, so we went
round the corner to a café called The Well.

Once we'd got our coffee, she introduced herself as Meg
and asked me about my relationship with Jesus. I told her I
knew about him but I didn't go to church. Then she asked

me if I knew I was a sinner. I nearly fell off my chair laughing. 'I've got enough sins to fill a book,' I told her. 'Do you want to start writing it?'

I did tell Meg how I'd become interested in the Bible when I was finishing off my last prison sentence and, as we finished our coffee, she said she'd like to pray with me. She explained that it would be a sinner's prayer, asking Jesus to forgive me my sins and to make me clean through his death on the cross for me. I said I was ready and the prayer went like this, 'Dear Lord Jesus, I come to you as a sinner and ask you to forgive me my sins. I believe you are the Son of God who died and rose again on the third day. Wash me and cleanse me by the power of your blood. Help me to start a new life with you and follow you in your ways. Today I receive you as my Lord and Saviour. In Jesus' name, Amen.'

It was 16 August 1995 when I said that prayer with Meg and meant it. It was a day I will remember for the rest of my life. At last I acknowledged to myself that I couldn't sink much lower, and that the drink and drugs were just my way of trying to escape from the reality of my life.

Meg gave me her address and the name of an hotel where she and her friends held a Sunday service. She told me that on Friday nights they met outside McDonalds in Victoria Street to sing and give out leaflets. After she left the café I put the slip of paper with all the details on it in my pocket and went back to my pitch hoping to sell more copies of *The Big Issue*. At the end of the afternoon, instead of going to the off-licence for my usual cans of cider, I went back home and searched through my bags to find the Bible Tina had given me in prison. In the two months since my release I'd forgotten all I learned in the Bible studies at Blundestone. I spent the night looking through the Bible, trying to find something to read that I would understand. For some reason Geoff and Kylie didn't call round that evening, so I was uninterrupted, but when morning came, I concluded that the Bible still didn't make much sense to me.

Two days later I gave it another go, but it was hopeless. I read the words on the page, but they meant nothing to me. I decided to go and see Meg and ask for her help. I scrubbed my jeans in the bath and washed my shirt, thinking that, if I was going to this Christian woman's nice home, I'd better make an effort. My bedsit was like me, not dirty but a bit of a mess.

I called at the address Meg had given me and the door was answered by a guy of about twenty. He looked as scruffy as me and it occurred to me that I might have the wrong address, but he confirmed that Meg lived there and I followed him into the flat. There was no carpet on the floor and the furniture was as tatty as mine, but Meg's welcome was warm and sincere. She was staying at the flat which belonged to Mel, the bloke who'd let me in.

As Meg prepared some soup, I chatted to Mel and discovered that he'd experienced plenty of tough times. He'd been homeless and spent long stretches in hospitals for the mentally ill. He'd been living rough when he became a Christian only seven weeks earlier, and in that brief time his life had been radically changed. He'd even succeeded in giving up smoking, something I wanted to do but wouldn't admit to! The four of us talked about the Bible and at the end of the evening Meg reminded me that they'd be outside McDonalds in Victoria Street the next evening. If I couldn't join them there, she added, she'd love me to call around on Sunday and go to church with them.

That Friday evening I stayed in, expecting Geoff to turn up. As I waited I read the stories in the Bible I remembered from Sunday School days. Before I realized it two hours had passed and there was no sign of Geoff, so I decided to go to Victoria Street and have a chat with Meg. There was a group of about ten outside McDonalds. They'd set up a generator to power an electric guitar and a mike and soon the singing was in full swing. I offered to help give out leaflets, but I didn't have any takers! Back in my bedsit I smoked a few joints, then had one pipe of puff before crashing out.

The next morning, after a breakfast of cornflakes and a pipe, I rolled the rest of my puff in a two skinner joint, then collected twenty copies of *The Big Issue* and bought a ticket to Dartford. On an average Saturday I'd sell all the copies and take about £20. This Saturday, when I went into Tie Rack to change up my cash, I found I'd taken £35. That was enough to buy puff for myself and for Willy who was still in prison. On the way home I decided to stop off in Deptford and visit Ken who'd been in prison with us. He'd always said that if I was going to see Willy, he'd give me a bit of puff on top to take in for him. When I got to Ken's flat he was so drunk he could hardly stand up and he hadn't got any puff. I told him not to worry, I'd get some in Victoria.

When I reached Victoria, I headed straight for the tube and made my way to Geoff and Kylie's. They told me they hadn't been to see me because Geoff had been ill for a week. He still looked pretty bad and I didn't stay long because they weren't able to supply me with any puff and I needed to get some sorted out because I wanted to go and see Willy the next day. I went to every dealer I knew in the Chalk Farm area, but they were either out or didn't have anything to sell me. I went back to Victoria and tried my regular supplier, the bloke in the flat below me. There was no answer. I went to the nearest phone box and started to ring around.

Finally, I got through to a guy who said he'd call round with some puff. Two hours went by and he still hadn't turned up. I called him again. No reply. I tried his mobile. It was switched off. I rang every half an hour, always with the same result. It was like going to the pub and not being able to buy a drink. I was angry and on edge because I couldn't even have a joint myself. I crawled into bed feeling that the whole world had let me down.

Sunday morning dawned, and I had to get some puff before ten o'clock when the coach left for the Isle of Wight and Albany prison. I tried the guy downstairs and the one who'd promised to come round. Neither responded, so I gave up on the plan to go and see Willy, and decided instead to visit the church Meg had talked about. I called at Mel's flat and we walked together to a hotel where the Holy Nation Church held its services. It seemed a strange venue, but it was very friendly and informal.

The pastor welcomed everyone there, especially first timers, and he seemed to be looking straight at me when he said it. Then the congregation launched into song, accompanied by people on the electric keyboard and guitar. I didn't know what they were singing, but there was one easy one called 'We are the winners' and I joined in. When we sang the line 'Satan defeated, Hallelujah!' I suddenly felt at peace. Tears rolled down my cheeks. By the time the singing ended I had a smile on my face and joy in my heart. I remember nothing of the sermon that day, but after the service Meg gave me an audio tape and asked me to listen to it at home.

I slipped the tape into the deck and listened through headphones. A man called Ian McCormack told his story.

He was stung by four box jelly fish while swimming in the Indian Ocean. The medical team worked hard, but Ian was pronounced dead and efforts at resuscitation ceased. Fifteen minutes later, to the shocked delight of those present, he revived. His tape, called *A Glimpse of Eternity* is an account of those fifteen minutes during which he was shown part of Heaven and Hell. I was so engrossed by Ian's story that I lost all sense of time and place. When the tape finished and I came back down to earth, I realized that I hadn't even had a roll-up that day. I picked up my tobacco and a packet of Rizlas and made one. After two drags, I nearly threw up. 'That's going to have to go,' I thought to myself and I took the tobacco to the rubbish chute outside my bedsit and threw it out. As I walked back inside, tears trickled down my face and the Holy Spirit filled my heart. I threw out my ashtrays and the empty cider cans, and made a decision to clean up the bedsit and sort myself out.

I went to the church office the next day and joined in the morning prayer. Everyone was praying in tongues, which was new to me but I wasn't bothered by it. I just knelt down and asked Jesus to help me sort out my life. I told the pastor I wanted to be rid of all the hash pipes and bongs, including the ones which belonged to Geoff. The pastor advised me not to throw away someone else's property, and suggested I returned Geoff's stuff to him. I was worried that if I went round to Geoff's I might be tempted to buy some drugs off him, so I put his bits into a carrier bag and stored them in a cupboard.

I was full of energy, like having a hit of speed. At three in the morning, I was chucking away pornographic magazines along with everything else I felt was bad. Even my little puff pipe that I had smoked every night before going to bed had to go. It was an act of repentance, although I didn't know it at the time. That evening I had dinner at Mel's flat, and when I got home I wrote to Willy. I told him about my plan to visit, how I'd been unable to buy puff anywhere and what had happened when I went to church instead of the Albany prison. I explained about feeling washed clean, which reminded me of the time when Georgy had visited me in the Verne, and I said I'd changed and hoped Willy would too. Finally I said I couldn't get up to visit him and that I'd given up taking drugs, but was sending him a postal order for £10 and would send him some more money when I could.

I put Willy's letter aside and took a fresh piece of paper. I wrote, 'Dear Mum and Dad' and stopped. What should I write? 'I know I haven't contacted you for ten tears but I've just met Jesus!' I tried to think it through. Did they still live at the same address? Were they still both alive? Would they believe I'd changed? I crumpled up the piece of paper and threw it in the bin. Writing to them was a crazy idea. I began to have doubts about sending Willy's letter. Perhaps I should go and see him instead. I decided to sleep on it.

I was up at 6 am saying my prayers for the third morning in a row. As I prayed I started to cry, but afterwards I was full of energy again. I leapt into the bath and said out loud, 'Lord you've cleaned me inside, I'll clean the outside.' After my bath and breakfast, I got to work on the bedsit. I was cleaning the windows when the postman came, and I smiled and said 'Good morning' to him. He smiled at me and said 'Good morning' back. Such a simple, unremarkable exchange and yet it felt like the best morning of my life. An hour or so later, as I was on my way to buy my copies of *The Big Issue*, I found the list of drug dealers' phone numbers in my pocket. I ripped it up and dumped it in a bin.

I arrived for morning prayers at the church office and joined the small group who gathered there at ten every day. Some of them would go out on the streets afterwards, preaching and singing. Meg worked on the computer, and Sophie cleaned the office and made drinks. Before I left for my pitch I showed my letter to Willy to the pastor. He thought I should send it, but I said nothing about the letter to my parents, although it was constantly on my mind.

When I returned to my bedsit, having sold my quota of *The Big Issue*, I realized that Geoff and Kylie hadn't been over since I met Meg. I laughed out loud as I pictured Geoff's face if he saw the state of the bedsit now. It was spotlessly clean and tidy. That night I prayed that God would give me the gift of tongues. Something welled up inside me, and a faint noise seemed to flow out of me from my throat, but nothing else happened. I went to bed feeling totally relaxed and at peace. It was very different the next morning. When I tried to repeat the experience I was almost physically sick. Determined to carry on, I knelt with my head over the toilet! I kept retching, as if I was going to vomit, but after a few minutes I felt better. At morning prayer it happened again. As I prayed, I shook and retched, but I didn't stop. Suddenly I felt full of energy. The words flowed and afterwards I realized that God had given me the gift I'd asked for.

A few of us went off to Little Ben. Mel took the mike and told how Jesus had saved him, then I spoke in public for the first time ever. I was brief and to the point. I said I knew nothing, except Christ and that he was crucified for me. Just three days ago I was doing drugs, but now Jesus had set me free. From being a prisoner I'd become a preacher! After that first experience of speaking on the streets, I went out regularly with the others, giving my testimony and handing out leaflets. I used to keep some of these on display in the bedsit, and when I found a sticker Tina had given me in Blundestone prison I stuck it on the bare light bulb. It was yellow with a smiley face printed on it and the words 'Smile, Jesus loves you.'

The next day I met the man who had been led to set up the Holy Nation Church. His name was Pastor Kunle Omilana, and he and his wife Rebecca had just returned from America. I poured out my story to him and he listened intently. I hadn't the faintest idea about church planting or how churches are organized, all I knew was that here was another person who not only had time for me but valued me too.

I was back in Dartford selling *The Big Issue*, at my usual Saturday pitch, when I collapsed. The woman from Tie Rack phoned for an ambulance. She thought I was having an epileptic seizure. I woke in hospital and the medical staff told me they could find nothing wrong with me, and no reason why I'd lost consciousness so dramatically. I told the doctor I'd recently become a Christian, and maybe I'd been delivered from something demonic. He told me he'd heard of such occurrences but discharged me with a clean bill of health. It has never happened since and may have been my body's reaction to being totally cut off from drugs.

When I returned to my bedsit after the evening service the following day, I wrote that letter to my parents and posted it to the last address I knew of, hoping they hadn't moved in the intervening decade. With that accomplished, I took the carrier bag of pipes and bongs over to Chalk Farm. I sat in Kylie's flat explaining to Geoff what had happened in my life. The more I talked, the more annoyed he became. When I said I'd thrown out everything I had to do with drugs, he said he wished I'd given them to him instead as he'd have found a use for them. He tersely brought the conversation to a close, saying he'd come over to collect the rent once a week.

Although losing Geoff as a friend didn't bother me too much, when I received a letter from Willy the next morning all the joy and energy my new life had given me drained away. The gist of the letter was that he thought I was a strong personality, not the type to be swayed by religion. He said I'd let him down and he was in debt because I hadn't come with the drugs. What really hurt me, though, was his statement: 'Don't try and convert me or I'll grow to hate you.'

He told me not to show his letter to anyone in the church, but I was feeling so bad about it that I took it to one of the blokes I went out witnessing with. He read it and said he would help me write a reply if I wanted him to. After morning prayers I came to a decision. I wouldn't write back to Willy. Any debts he'd incurred were down to him, not me. Once again I thought of Georgy telling me he'd become a Christian, and how I'd told him that he was wasting a visit by not bringing in any drugs. If a friendship was based solely on drugs, I concluded, it wasn't a genuine friendship. Pastor Mike confirmed my feelings. He read Willy's letter and afterwards said that when we decide to follow Jesus, there will be some things and some people whom we have to leave behind us. We shouldn't forget them, but should go on praying for them. As I went off to sell *The Big Issue*, I ripped up Willy's letter and threw it in the bin.

My tattoos were another worry. I had heard that Satan can attack where there are demonic signs, but I hadn't a chance of raising enough money to have them removed. Some of the people at church put my mind at rest. They told me that when we come to Jesus Christ, he breaks every curse or stronghold that Satan has over us, because Jesus came to destroy the works of the Devil. Meg prayed with me and denounced all the bad things connected with the tattoos. Now I use the tattoos to show that Jesus can indeed triumph over the Devil and turn a person's life around.

Satan doesn't give up easily. For me the battle had only just begun. I started to settle in my new routine – daily morning prayers with Mel, Meg, Sophie, Wally and Pastor Mike; preaching on the streets twice a week and selling *The Big Issue* every day except for Sunday. But nothing stays the same. Meg had to leave London and I felt that, just as I had found a true friend who really cared about me, God was sending her away. We held a going-away party for Meg, and the following night I sat alone in my bedsit with a couple of cans of cider. Looking round, I thought of all the stuff I'd thrown out. Without Meg, I mused, it was all for nothing. There was a knock on the door. I knew it would be Meg, but I wouldn't let myself open the door. She kept knocking and I could hear her calling 'Mick', but I didn't move out of my chair. In the end she gave up and left. When I woke up the next morning I felt empty. I went to the church office, and as I prayed I realized that Satan had robbed me of the joy of saying goodbye to Meg at the station. The Bible says that Satan is a thief who comes to kill, steal and destroy, and I had just found out that what he wants to steal from you most isn't possessions but love, peace and happiness. That morning I recovered the joy in my life.

I decided to leave the bedsit and move in with Mel. I went to Chalk Farm to tell Geoff that I was moving out at the end of the week. I had the distinct impression that he wanted me out anyway. I told him I'd cleaned it up and when he came to pick up the keys he was visibly impressed with what I'd done. I'd already shifted all my belongings to Mel's flat so I walked away leaving only one small reminder of my time there – a sticker on the light bulb saying, 'Smile, Jesus loves you!'

Light from a Dark star

Wayne Kirkland

There are no simple answers to the big question: 'If God is a God of love, who does he allow so much pain and suffering?'

Wayne Kirkland does not attempt to shrug off the serious challenges to faith which the question raises. Rather he faces the problems head on and sets them out in sharp relief. He offers a compassionate engaging of the suffering of real people, a grappling with the slippery issues and discovers some intriguing perspectives.

Described by Michael Green as the most accessible book of suffering he has ever read.

Wayne Kirkland lives and works in New Zealand.

Scripture Union
ISBN: 1-85999-515-2

Price: £4.99

£3.99 with money off voucher

Chapter 1

My diary of pain

Thursday 1:00am

The phone rings – that distant, insistent jangle that drags me from deep sleep. 'It must be some ungodly hour,' I think to myself as I stumble through to the study, ready to give the caller a piece of my mind. I look at the clock. It's 1:00am.

The voice is instantly familiar. 'It's Dad here, Wayne. Sorry to ring you at this time of the night...but I have some very, very bad news. I don't know how to tell you this... Your brother... it's Phil... he's killed himself.'

Quick as that. The words only take a few seconds. My life is never going to be the same again.

The news starts to sink in. Not just shock – sheer panic and terror! Like a knife to my heart. I find myself struggling for breath. My wife Jill is at my side in the study by this time, asking in a frightened voice what's wrong. As I stammer my bewildered questions to Dad she must be gaining some idea.

The rest of the call is brief. I get off the phone, tell Jill and burst into tears. I don't know what to do. I walk downstairs, gasping as I try to take it all in. Cries come from the pit of my stomach – deep, shuddering sobs.

I know instinctively that this is going to be a very long night. Jill rings good friends and they offer to come immediately.

People? People coming? My first thought is to shower and dress!

It's a knee-jerk reaction, but it does help. I need to do something physical, just to cope with the horror of it all. And it also gives me a few minutes by myself. My sobbing doesn't stop in the shower. Painful convulsions of horror and disbelief.

Thursday 4:30am
Over 200 miles to our home town. In his typical fatherly fashion Dad said not to do anything until the morning, but that's a forlorn hope! For an hour I function on 'auto pilot' while Jill and I pack everything we need and load the car. Then, when it's all ready, we wake our three children and tell them what has happened. Within minutes we're in the car, on our way.

Jill tells me to let her know when I want her to take the wheel, but driving keeps my mind active. As we come closer to New Plymouth I think about what we'll find. I feel like turning and driving away, but I know I can't.

Thursday 8:30am
A beautiful, fine, summer morning – and no way of enjoying it. We open the front gate, walk up the path and round to the back of the house. There we peer through the French doors. Someone sees us and unfastens the lock. Inside it's like a battlefield. Bodies on the floor, slumped on chairs... dazed and silent.

Phil's wife, Jo, has just told her three children that their Daddy is dead.

Friday

Waking up brings an avalanche of dreadful feelings. Another warm, sunny morning but I can't celebrate it. Everyone else is the same. Mum and Dad have been up since 4am, talking and crying together, going back over Phil's life.

I walk out onto the back porch. I sit down with Mum and Jill to read the death notices in the morning paper. That simple act brings perhaps the saddest moment I have ever experienced.

There in black and white – the bald statement that my kid brother is dead. This is the end. Utter desolation. We weep and weep.

Saturday

The day of the funeral. We've been preparing ourselves for this moment for two days now. I wish I could attend the service without having to meet anyone, but I know I have to face people. The church is packed to overflowing. Friends have come from everywhere.

The service is a blur, except for a stunning poem by Craig – Phil's business partner: *Phil, you flamed our lives with golden laughter...*

The walk behind the coffin seems a million miles. Everyone is shattered and distraught. Questions. Endless questions.

And so few answers...

Wednesday – one week later

Cricket at the park is soothing – yet another chance to think. But always I come back to the reality that this time last week Phil was alive. Alive and in pain. I wish again and again that I could go back to that week. That I could be with him and talk to him and stop him from doing such an awful thing.

Dinner with family, but I'm bad company. During the meal I keep watching the clock and thinking of each step in the chain of events, the final countdown that's revealed by the phone record:

5:45pm: last inward fax.
5:55pm: returned fax.
6:15–6:30pm: last incoming phone call.

That's all we have to go on. Phil was probably dead by 7pm.

It's quarter to seven now.

I can't take it any longer. I leave, driving to Phil's place of work. Here's where he hanged himself, not to be found for several hours. I walk round the building and think, 'Oh Phil, if only I'd known, if only I was there'.

Suicide seems to make our grieving so much more complicated. If Phil had died in a genuine accident, we could have coped better. Knowing he was in peace, we would only have our own grief and sense of loss to bear... not that untouchable ocean of despair which must have been his. Everything is clouded by the knowledge that this was a conscious choice, the result of Phil's inward hurt and unhappiness.

And we weren't there. He died by himself. No one to witness it. No one to mourn. That's painful. That's excruciatingly painful.

Finally I say my goodbyes, as if it's last week, then drive back along country roads, trying to make sense of it all.

It seemed as bad as it could be, but it wasn't. I think suffering must feed on suffering.

In the months after Phil's death the cloud of despair that wrapped itself around me started to clear a little. Life was beginning to return to some sense of normality. I was looking ahead for the first time with real hope.

And then this...

Sunday night, almost six months later

An exhausting day. Getting close to bedtime and we've been out, so I decide to check the answerphone messages. There's one from Dad. His voice sounds awfully wavery – like something's seriously wrong. He wants me to call him. I do, straight away.

Dad answers and when he discovers who it is he says, 'I've got some more bad news, Wayne. Your cousin Mark has done the same thing as Phil. They found him last night.'

Stunned is not a strong enough word to describe my emotions. I'm overwhelmed with the sense that I have lived through this moment before. I can't believe it. What's happening? Is our family coming apart at the seams?

Wednesday morning, 11:30am

We arrive in the small town where my cousin lived with his family. It's been a long journey – this one even more cruel than the last.

We meet Mum and Dad for lunch in the main street. Still a couple of hours before the funeral. We begin to talk. I can see the pain in their eyes. Actually, it's more than pain. It's fear. They don't speak about it, but it's there. Are either of their remaining Sons going to take the same option?

I voice the reassurance they so desperately need to hear. I have no intention of leaving them to deal with even more loss and pain. It's not an option. Never will be.

The relief streams back into their faces and we try to cope with this new grief together.

Wednesday, a week later

Life goes on... and yet the questions still remain. Why?
Why? Why?

Chapter 2

A planet in pain

The truth of the matter is that all we have to do is live long enough and we will suffer.

Don Carson

We live in a hurting world. If you've managed to avoid tragedy this far, you're in the minority. From the ease of our comfortable suburbs, the pain may seem distant. We may even for a time deny that life is generally difficult – in fact, grindingly difficult – for most of the six billion inhabitants of Planet Earth. But the truth is, despite the huge advances our civilisation has made, existence for vast numbers of people is more often brutish than civilised, more filled with despair, agony and suffering than it is with hope, joy and fulfilment.

Of course, it's easy to be seduced into thinking that extreme suffering only happens in someone else's back-yard, far removed from our own slice of heaven. Easy, that is, until we're confronted with it face-on; until it happens to a friend, family member, neighbour or workmate. It may be incurable cancer, a road death, a tragic accident; a pain-filled disease...

And how many go through suffering-by-association as

they watch a loved one waste away with Alzheimer's or MS or AIDS?

To live is to suffer – one of life's primal lessons. None of us escapes it. None of us is a stranger to pain. I'm certainly not. So far I've been spared the physical hurts and disabilities that some people endure but, like everyone else, I've gone through times of misery that have scarred my soul.

We all do. And nobody knows why!

We grow up with suffering. It's part of the world we belong to, and we take it for granted. Until one day the awfulness hits us... and then the questions burst out.

> Where does suffering come from?
> Who causes it?
> How come some people suffer far more than others, more than they ever deserve?
> Why can't we have a world without all this anguish and heartache?

You've chosen to pick up this book. You've been interested enough to read it this far as I've re-lived my own little chunk of misery. I guess that means *you* wonder about this whole thing, too. Maybe you have the same questions I do? Maybe you're like a number of people I've met. When they hear that I take seriously my faith in God, they buttonhole me and abuse me (mostly in a friendly way!), complaining about what God has done or failed to do in their own lives. Or just generally sounding off about this messy world...

Are You Listening?

Nick Fawcett

Do you find prayer easy? When talking directly to God, do you struggle for words? Even after years as a minister, Nick Fawcett finds there are still times when he cries out for answers and finds only silence.

Yet prayer is meant to be the expression of a relationship – a dialogue where the answers are often found in Scripture.

This is a collection of prayers primarily for personal devotion. Starting with the emotions we encounter in daily life, Nick Fawcett has turned to the Bible as a way to understanding what God would say to us.

Nick Fawcett is a freelance writer and Toc H worker.

Kevin Mayhew Limited
ISBN: 1-84003-308-8

Price: £10.50

£8.50 with money off voucher

Introduction

Do you find prayer easy? I don't. Though I have led prayer in worship for many years, when it comes to talking directly to God I often find myself struggling for words. And, through my experience as a minister, I know that many feel the same. Whilst at times, for us all, prayer can be a huge blessing, at others it can become little more than a duty, even a chore.

So why? Well, perhaps one reason is that we make prayer too formal. There is nothing wrong with that in the context of public worship – indeed there it is probably necessary, but when it comes to personal devotion it's different. Prayer is meant to be the expression of a relationship, not an exercise in composition or grammar, and that should mean we feel able to be honest to God, free to bring before him the things that matter to us, the good and the bad, the joys and the sorrows, the hopes and the fears. That's what this collection of prayers aims to help us do. It starts from daily life and brings before God the emotions which are part of it – fear, hope, joy, sorrow, excitement, anxiety, and countless others. Each is offered openly to him.

But, of course, prayer doesn't end with us, or at least it shouldn't do. It is meant to be about dialogue – here perhaps is another reason some of us struggle with it, because it can all too often seem anything but. We may speak glibly about prayer being a conversation – even, as one children's chorus puts it, like a telephone – but in reality it's not. We've all had times when we pour out our souls and it's like staring into a black hole, when we cry out for an answer and find only silence, when we look for guidance but find none forthcoming. Yet it may be that the answer is there more often than we might think, if only we know where to look – and where better than in the Scriptures? So often, when we turn to the Bible, it is as if to find words written expressly for us, offering the answer we are looking for, the message we so urgently need to hear. It is this that lies behind the second part of each prayer in this collection. I do not presume in any way to set myself up as God, but rather to make suggestions, based upon Bible passages, which may open the way to understanding what God would say to us.

All the material in this book is written primarily for use in personal devotion, though some could effectively be used in public worship, one person reading the first part of each prayer, and another the second. Everything I have written is inevitably coloured by my own ideas and experiences, but it is also a reflection of the joys and sorrows, the hopes and inspirations of so many I have been privileged to know during the course of my ministry. I hope it may also be a reflection of life for you, and some help in leading to a deeper and more personal encounter with God.

Nick Fawcett

Chapter 1

It's me, O Lord

What sort of language should we use in prayer? What sort of subjects are appropriate to bring before God? Most of us would probably find questions like these hard to answer, for our response would almost certainly depend on what we were praying for and how we were feeling at the time. Occasionally prayer simply flows, our innermost feelings finding expression naturally and spontaneously. But there are times also when we approach prayer almost mechanically, saying what we think God wants to hear rather than what we really want to tell him. Why? Partly, I think, because there lurks in many of us a vague sense that prayer requires a special sort of language, almost a technical expertise, if God is to hear us. But perhaps the main reason is that we feel some matters are best kept to ourselves. Yet if prayer is to nurture our faith and our growth as individuals, to become a dialogue rather than a monologue, we need to be honest with God and bring ourselves as we are with no holds barred.

Two men went up to the temple to pray, one a Pharisee and the other a tax collector. The Pharisee, standing by himself was praying thus, 'God, I thank you that I am not like other people: thieves, rogues,

*adulterers, or even like this tax collector. I fast twice a week; I give a
tenth of all my income.' But the tax collector, standing far off would
not even look up to heaven, but was beating his breast and saying,
'God, be merciful to me, a sinner!'*

Luke 18:10-13

*Simon Peter fell down at Jesus' knees, saying, 'Go away from me,
Lord, for I am a sinful man!'*

Luke 5:8

It's me, O Lord:
    not the person I pretend to be,
    nor who I want to be,
    but me, as I am,
    with all my strengths,
    all my weaknesses,
    all my faith,
    all my doubt –
    me, as I've rarely dared come before,
    reaching out to you in prayer.
I've no right to be here, I know that,
    for I'm nothing special,
    nothing to write home about,
    and I've little idea what I'm going to say,
    still less how to say it.
But you tell us if we truly seek, we shall find,
    if we're really sorry, you'll forgive,
    if we keep on asking, you will answer.
So I'm here, Lord,
    in all my ugliness and sin –
    weak,
    selfish,
    greedy,

thoughtless –
but I'm here,
and I'm asking you, despite it all:
hear my prayer.

My child,
  don't stop,
  keep talking,
  for I'm here too,
  delighted to listen,
  drinking in your every word.
It's a joy to hear you, believe me,
  music to my ears –
  no need to apologise or excuse yourself.
I've looked forward to this moment for so long,
  your coming openly and honestly to meet me.
For it's *you* I want to talk to –
  not the mask you wear for the world;
  you as you really are –
  the face you show, the face you hide,
  the person you love, the person you hate.
They're both you,
  two halves of the same whole,
  inseparable as light and dark, substance and shadow,
  and unless you bring all,
  openly and honestly before me,
  you bring nothing.
You're not perfect – I know that –
  but I don't ask you to be;
  it's not me who twists the knife, only yourself.
I love you as you are,
  with all your faults and fragile faith,
  and I'll go on loving you day after day,

drawing you closer to me
not as a condition but an expression of that love.
So come now, gladly and confidently,
    bring yourself with head bent low but soul held
        high,
    and find in me your kindest critic
    and truest friend.

*Ask, and it will be given to you; search, and you will find; knock, and
the door will be opened for you. For everyone who asks receives, and
everyone who searches finds, and for everyone who knocks, the door
will be opened.*

Matthew 7:7-8

*If we say that we have no sin, we deceive ourselves, and the truth is not
in us. If we confess our sins, he who is faithful and just will forgive us
our sins and cleanse us from all unrighteousness.*

1 John 1:8-9

Chapter 14

Why, Lord?

Of all the mysteries of life and faith, none is harder to reconcile than the problem of suffering. How is it, we ask, that a supposedly loving and caring God can allow so much pain and misery to rack our world? Across the centuries greater minds than mine have wrestled with this conundrum yet failed to come up with a complete answer, and no doubt many more will do the same in years to come. There are no easy words or comfortable solutions – only the conviction of faith that God is there within our sorrow, sharing the pain, experiencing the grief, reaching out to the broken, suffering with those who suffer. For reasons we cannot fathom, such things are an integral part of creation which even God himself is caught up in, until that day when there will be no more pain, no more tears, and he will be all in all.

> *Why, O Lord, do you stand far off? Why do you hide yourself in times of trouble?*
>
> Psalm 10:1

My God, my God, why have you forsaken me? Why are you so far from helping me, from the words of my groaning? O my God, I cry by day, but you do not answer; and by night, but find no rest.

Psalm 22:1-2

Why did I not die at birth, come forth from the womb and expire? Now I would be lying down and quiet; I would be asleep; then I would be at rest. Why is light given to one in misery, and life to the bitter in soul, who long for death, but it does not come? Why is light given to the one who cannot see the way, whom God has fenced in? For my sighing comes like my bread, and my groanings are poured out like water. Truly the thing that I fear comes upon me, and what I dread befalls me. I am not at ease, nor am I quiet; I have no rest; but trouble comes.

Job 3:11, 13, 20-21a, 23-26

Why, Lord?
I know I shouldn't ask that,
    but I just can't help it,
    for I'm troubled,
        unable to make sense of this faith of mine,
        unable to make sense of anything.
It doesn't worry me usually,
    for I can avoid the issues,
        thankful that they don't touch me,
        not yet anyway.
But today I've been surrounded by suffering,
    by the sheer weight of human need,
        and it's got to me in a way it rarely has before.
I visited the hospital,
    and saw my friend there in the cancer ward,
        curled up in bed,
        eyes sunken,

teeth gritted against the pain –
the operation over, but the prognosis grim.
I left him, blinking back the tears,
    but there were others,
    so many others,
    looking across the ward at me
    with pain, fear and sorrow in their eyes.
I went on to the nursing home to see another friend,
    once so vibrant, so full of life,
    but now her mind gone, her body withered –
    a mocking shadow of her former self,
    waiting for the merciful release of death.
I was glad to leave, Lord,
    glad to get out into the fresh air away from it all;
    but then an ambulance raced past, sirens blaring,
    a drunken vagrant stumbled by the roadside,
    and across the street a young boy grimaced in a
        wheelchair,
    limbs twisted, mouth dribbling.
It was everywhere,
    human suffering crying out in defiant protest –
    on the front of the newspaper,
    the car radio, the television news –
    another murder, another rape,
    another war, another tragedy;
    and suddenly, Lord, as I stared starkly into the
        darkness,
    I could hold it back no longer –
    the inevitable question:
    why?

My child,
  don't be ashamed of asking,
  for I don't blame you,
  not in the slightest.
On the contrary, my only surprise is that it took you
      so long,
  for it's not as it should be, this world I've made,
  not as I want it,
  nor as I planned it.
I look upon it day after day,
  the pain and sorrow,
  the hatred and cruelty,
  and it breaks my heart to see the beauty I intended
  so cruelly disfigured,
  laughter turning to despair,
  joy into tragedy.
That's why I came through my Son,
  sharing your humanity and bearing your sorrow –
  to ensure that one day it will be different,
  the time coming when there will be no more
      suffering,
  tears or darkness.
It will come, believe me,
  but the time must be right,
  and, until then, as well as joy there must be sorrow,
  as well as pleasure, pain,
  as well as life, death,
  each a part of a fallen, broken world.
Yet seen or unseen,
  recognised or unrecognised,
  I am there with you,
  not watching from the sidelines, casually aloof,
  nor safely at a distance, untouched and unmoved,

but sharing in your hurt,
   aching with those who ache,
   groaning with those who groan,
   weeping with those who weep.
I cannot stop your pain,
   but I can help bear it,
   and though you'll still have doubts and still ask
      why,
   I can only say:
   hold on to me,
   as I keep hold of you.

*Rise up, O Lord; O God, lift up your hand; do not forget the op-
pressed. You do see! Indeed, you note trouble and grief that you may
take it into your hands; the helpless commit themselves to you.*

Psalm 10:12, 14

*I am utterly bowed down and prostrate; all day long I go around
mourning. For my loins are filled with burning, and there is no sound-
ness in my flesh. I am utterly spent and crushed; I groan because of the
tumult of my heart. O Lord, all my longing is known to you; my sighing is not hidden from you. My heart throbs, my strength fails me; as
for the light of my eyes — it also has gone from me. My friends and com-
panions stand aloof from my affliction, and my neighbours stand afar
off. But it is for you, O Lord, that I wait; it is you, O Lord my God,
who will answer. Do not forsake me, O Lord; O my God, do not be
far from me; make haste to help me, O Lord, my salvation.*

Psalm 38:6–11, 15, 21–22

Victory Over the Darkness

Neil T. Anderson

Every day millions of Christians live below par – emotionally, physically, and spiritually. Because they do not grasp the central fact of their identity in Christ, they miss out on the freedom and maturity they should enjoy.

Dr Anderson seeks to redress the balance. In this revised and updated edition with current illustrations, he encourages all who long for spiritual growth.

'If you see yourself as a child of God who is spiritually alive in Christ, you'll begin to live in victory and freedom.'

President of Freedom in Christ Ministries, Dr Anderson is a bestselling author, pastor and teacher.

Monarch Books
ISBN: 1-85424-498-1

Price: £6.99

£4.99 with money off voucher

Monarch Books, Concorde House, Grenville Place, Mill Hill, London,
NW7 3SA

Introduction
Lend Me Your Hope

Several years ago in my first pastorate, I committed myself to disciple a young man in my church. It was my first formal attempt at one-on-one discipling. Russ and I decided to meet early every Tuesday morning so I could lead him through an inductive Bible study on the topic of love. We both began with high hopes. Russ was looking forward to taking some major steps of growth as a Christian, and I was eager to help him develop into a mature believer.

Six months later we were still slogging through the same inductive Bible study on love. We weren't getting anywhere. For some reason, our Paul-and-Timothy relationship wasn't working. Russ didn't seem to be growing as a Christian. He felt defeated and I felt responsible for his defeat — but I didn't know what else to do. Our once high hopes for Russ's great strides toward maturity had gradually deflated like a balloon with a slow leak. We eventually stopped meeting together.

Two years later, after I had moved to another pastorate, Russ came to see me. He poured out the story of what had been going on in his life during our brief one-on-one relationship – a story that revealed a secret part of his life I never knew existed. Russ was deeply involved in sin and unwilling to share his struggle with me. I could sense that he wasn't free, but I had no clue why this was the case.

At that time, I had little experience with people in the bondage of sin and was determined to plough on. I thought the major problem was just his unwillingness to complete the material. Now, however, I am convinced that my attempts at discipling Russ failed for another reason.

The apostle Paul wrote, 'I gave you milk to drink, not solid food; for *you were not yet able to receive it.* Indeed, even now *you are not yet able,* for you are still fleshly. For since there is jealousy and strife among you, are you not fleshly, and are you not walking like mere men?' (1 Cor. 3:2,3, emphasis added). Apparently, because of unresolved conflicts in their lives, carnal Christians are not able to receive the solid food of God's Word.

That's when I began to discern that discipling people to Christian maturity involves much more than leading them through a step-by-step, 10-week Bible study. We live in a country glutted with biblical material, Christian books, radio and television, but many Christians are not moving on to spiritual maturity. Some are no more loving now than they were 20 years ago. We read in 1 Timothy, 'The goal of our instruction is love from a pure heart and a good conscience and a sincere faith' (1:5).

Since that time the focus of my ministry, both as a pastor and a seminary professor, has been the interrelated ministries of discipling and Christian counseling. I have been a disciple and a counselor of countless people. I have also taught discipleship and pastoral counseling at the seminary level and in churches and leadership conferences across the country and around the world. I have found one common denominator for all struggling Christians. They do not know who they are in Christ, nor do they understand what it means to be a child of God. Why not? If 'The Spirit Himself bears witness with our spirit that we are children of God' (Rom. 8:16), why weren't they sensing it?

As a pastor, I believed that Christ was the answer and truth would set people free, but I really didn't know how. People at my church had problems for which I didn't have answers, but God did. When the Lord called me to teach at Talbot School of Theology, I was searching for answers myself. Slowly I began to understand how to help people resolve their personal and spiritual conflicts through genuine repentance by submitting to God and resisting the devil (see Jas. 4:7).

My seminary education had taught me about the kingdom of God, but not about the kingdom of darkness and that 'our struggle is not against flesh and blood, but against rulers, against the powers, against the world forces of this darkness, against the spiritual forces of wickedness in the heavenly places' (Eph. 6:12). Through countless hours of intense counseling with defeated Christians, I began to understand the battle for their minds and how they could be transformed by renewing their minds.

I am saddened by how we have separated the ministries of discipleship and counseling in our churches. Christian discipleship too often has become an impersonal program, although good theological material is being used. Christian counseling has been intensely personal, but often lacks good theology. I believe discipleship and counseling are biblically the same. If you were a good discipler you would be a good counselor and vice versa. Discipleship counseling is the process where two or more people meet together in the presence of Christ, learn how the truth of God's

Word can set them free and thus are able to conform to the image of God as they walk by faith in the power of the Holy Spirit.

In the course of learning this, my family. and I went through a very broken experience. For 15 months I didn't know whether my wife, Joanne, was going to live or die. We lost everything we had. God gave me something very dear to me that I could not fix. No matter what I did, nothing changed. God brought me to the end of my resources, so I could discover His. That was the birth of Freedom in Christ Ministries. Nobody reading this book knows any better than I do that I can't set anybody free; only God can do that. I can't bind up anybody's broken heart; only God can do that. He is the Wonderful Counselor. Brokenness is the key to effective ministry and the final ingredient for discipleship counseling. Message and method had come together.

Furthermore, it is my conviction that discipleship counseling must start where the Bible starts: We must have a true knowledge of God and know who we are as children of God. If we really knew God, our behavior would change radically and instantly. Whenever heaven opened to reveal the glory of God, individual witnesses in the Bible were immediately and profoundly changed. I believe that the greatest determinant of mental and spiritual health and spiritual freedom is a true understanding of God and a right relationship with Him. A good theology is an indispensable prerequisite to a good psychology.

Several weeks after one of my conferences, a friend shared with me the story of a dear Christian woman who had attended. She had lived in a deep depression for several years. She survived by leaning on her friends, three counseling sessions a week and a variety of prescription drugs.

During the conference this woman realized that her support system included everybody and everything but God. She had not cast her anxiety on Christ and she was anything but dependent on Him. She took her conference syllabus home and began focusing on her identity in Christ and expressing confidence in Him to meet her daily needs. She threw off all her other supports (a practice I do not recommend) and decided to trust in Christ alone to relieve her depression. She began living by faith and renewing her mind as the conference notes suggested. After one month she was a different person. Knowing God is indispensable to maturity and freedom.

Another point at which discipling and counseling intersect is in the area of individual responsibility. People who want to move forward in Christian maturity can certainly benefit from the counsel of others, and those who seek freedom from their past can also be helped by others. Ultimately, however, every Christian is responsible for his or her own maturity and freedom in Christ. Nobody can make you grow. That's your decision and daily responsibility. Nobody can solve your problems for you. You alone must initiate and follow through with that process. Thankfully, however, none of us walks through the disciplines of personal maturity and freedom alone. The indwelling Christ is eagerly willing to walk with us each step of the way.

This book is the first of two books I have written from my education and experience in discipling and counseling others. This book focuses on the foundational issues of living and maturing in Christ. You will discover who you are, in Christ and how to live by faith. You will learn how to walk by the Spirit and be sensitive to His leading. The grace walk is living by faith in the power of the Holy Spirit.

In this book you will discover the nature of the battle for your mind and learn why your mind must be transformed so you can live by faith and grow spiritually. You will gain insight into how to manage your emotions and be set free from the emotional traumas of your past through faith and forgiveness.

In my second book, *The Bondage Breaker* (Harvest House Publishers), I focus on our freedom in Christ and the spiritual conflicts that affect Christians today. Being alive and free in Christ is an essential prerequisite for maturity in Christ. We cannot achieve instant maturity. It will take us the rest of our lives to renew our minds and conform to the image of God, but it doesn't take as long to realize our identity and freedom in Christ. The world, the flesh and the devil are enemies of our sanctification, but they have been and can be overcome in Christ.

I suggest that you complete this book first, learn about living and growing in Christ, then work through the subjects of spiritual conflicts and freedom by reading *The Bondage Breaker.*

Victory over the Darkness is arranged something like a New Testament Epistle. The first half of the book lays a doctrinal foundation and defines terms that are necessary for understanding and implementing the more practical chapters that follow. You may be tempted to skip over the first half because it seems less relevant to daily experience. It is critical, however, to discern your position and victory in Christ so you can implement the practices of growth in Him. You need to know what to believe before you can understand what to do.

I have talked to thousands of people like Russ, my first discipleship candidate. They are Christians, but they are not growing and they are not bearing fruit. They want to serve Christ, but they can't seem to get over the top and get on with their lives in a meaningful and productive way. They need to have their hope reestablished in Christ, as the following poem describes:

> Lend me your hope for awhile,
>> I seem to have mislaid mine.
> Lost and hopeless feelings accompany me daily,
>> pain and confusion are my companions.
> I know not where to turn;
>> looking ahead to future times does not bring forth
>> images of renewed hope.
> I see troubled times, pain-filled days, and more
>> tragedy.
>
> Lend me your hope for awhile,
>> I seem to have mislaid mine.
> Hold my hand and hug me;
>> listen to all my ramblings, recovery seems so far
>> distant.
> The road to healing seems like a long and lonely one.
>
> Lend me your hope for awhile,
>> I seem to have mislaid mine.
> Stand by me, offer me your presence, your heart and
>> your love.
> Acknowledge my pain, it is so real and ever present.
> I am overwhelmed with sad and conflicting thoughts.
>
> Lend me your hope for awhile;
>> a time will come when I will heal,
>> and I will share my renewal,
>> hope and love with others.'

Do these words reflect your experience and echo your plea as a believer? Do you sometimes feel hemmed in by the world, the flesh and the devil to the point that you wonder if your Christianity is worth anything? Do you sometimes fear you will never be all God called you to be? Do you long to get on with your Christian maturity and experience the freedom God's Word promises?

I want to share my hope with you in the pages ahead. Your maturity is the product of time, pressure, trials, tribulations, the knowledge of God's Word, an understanding of who you are in Christ and the presence of the Holy Spirit in your life. You probably already have the first four elements in abundance; most Christians do. Let me add some generous doses of the last three ingredients. When Christians are alive and free in Christ, watch them grow!

Note

1. Adapted from the poem 'Lend Me Your Hope,' author unknown.

Chapter 1

Who Are You?

I really enjoy asking people, 'Who are you?' It sounds like a simple question requiring a simple answer, but it really isn't. For example, if someone asked me, 'Who are you?' I might answer, 'Neil Anderson.'

'No, that's your name. Who are you?'

'Oh, I'm a seminary professor.'

'No, that's what you do.' 'I'm an American.'

'That's where you live.' 'I'm an evangelical.'

'That's your denominational preference.'

I could also say that I am five feet nine inches tall and a little over 150 pounds — actually *quite* a little over 150 pounds! My physical dimensions and appearance, however, aren't me either. If you chopped off my arms and legs would I still be me? If you transplanted my heart, kidneys or liver would I still be me? Of course! Now if you keep chopping you will get to me eventually because I am in here somewhere. Who I am, though, is far more than what you see on the outside.

The apostle Paul said, 'We recognize no man according to the flesh' (2 Cor. 5:16). Maybe the Early Church didn't, but generally we do. We tend to identify ourselves and each other primarily by what we look like (tall, short, stocky, slender) or what we do (plumber, carpenter, nurse, engineer, clerk). Furthermore, when we Christians are asked to identify our selves in relation to our faith, we usually talk about our doctrinal position (Protestant, evangelical, Calvinist, charismatic), our denominational preference (Baptist, Presbyterian, Methodist, Independent) or our role in the church (Sunday School teacher, choir member, deacon, usher).

Is who you are determined by what you do, or is what you do determined by who you are? That is an important question, especially as it relates to Christian maturity. I subscribe to the latter. I believe that your hope for growth, meaning and fulfillment as a Christian is based on understanding who you are – specifically your identity in Christ as a child of God. Your understanding of who God is and who you are in relationship to Him is the critical foundation for your belief system and your behavior patterns as a Christian.

False Equations in the Search for identity

Several years ago a 17-year-old girl drove a great distance to talk with me. I have never met a girl who had so much going for her. She was cover-girl pretty and had a wonderful figure. She was immaculately dressed. She had completed 12 years of school in 11 years and graduated near the top of her class. As a talented musician, she had received a full-ride music scholarship to a Christian university. She also drove a brand-new sports car her parents gave her for graduation. I was amazed that one person could have so much.

She talked with me for half an hour and I realized that what I saw on the outside wasn't matching what I was beginning to see on the inside.

'Mary,' I said finally, 'have you ever cried yourself to sleep at night because you felt inadequate and wished you were somebody else?'

She began to cry. 'How did you know?'

'Truthfully, Mary,' I answered, 'I've learned that people who *appear* to have it all together on the outside may not have it all together on the inside. I could ask almost anyone that same question at some time in their lives and get the same response.'

Often what we show on the outside is a false front designed to disguise who we really are, and we cover up the negative feelings we have about ourselves. The world would have us believe that if we appear attractive or perform well or enjoy a certain amount of status, then we will have it all together inside as well. That is not always true, however. External appearance, accomplishment and recognition don't necessarily reflect – or produce – internal peace and maturity.

In his book *The Sensation of Being Somebody,* Maurice Wagner expresses this false belief in simple equations we tend to accept. He says we mistakenly think that good appearance plus the admiration it brings equal a whole person. Or we feel that star performance plus accomplishments equal a whole person. Or we believe that a certain amount of status plus the recognition we accumulate equal a whole person. Not so. These equations are no more correct than two plus two equal six. Wagner says:

> Try as we might by our appearance, performance or social status to find self-verification for a sense of being somebody, we always come short of satisfaction. Whatever pinnacle of self-identity we achieve soon crumbles under the pressure of hostile rejection or criticism, introspection or guilt, fear or

anxiety. We cannot do anything to qualify for the by-product
of being loved unconditionally and voluntarily.'

If these equations could work for anyone, they would have
worked for King Solomon. He was the king of Israel during the greatest years in its history. He had power, position,
wealth, possessions and women. If a meaningful life is the
result of appearance, admiration, performance, accomplishments, status or recognition, Solomon would have
been the most together man who ever lived.

Not only did he possess all that a fallen humanity could
hope for, but God also gave him more wisdom than any
other mortal to interpret it all. What was his conclusion?
'Meaningless! Meaningless!... Utterly meaningless!
Everything is meaningless' (Eccles. 1:2, NIV). Solomon
sought to find purpose and meaning in life independent of
God and he wrote a book about it. The book of Ecclesias-
tes describes the futility of humankind pursuing a meaningful life in a fallen world without God. Millions of
people climb those ladders of 'success,' only to discover
when they reach the top that their ladder is leaning against
the wrong wall.

We also tend to buy into the negative side of the worldly
success-equals-meaning formula by believing that if
people have nothing, they have no hope for happiness. For
example, I presented this scenario to a high school student
a few years ago: 'Suppose there's a girl on your campus who
has a potato body and stringy hair, who stumbles when she
walks and stutters when she talks. She has a bad complexion and she struggles just to get average grades. Does she
have any hope for happiness?'

He thought for a moment, then answered, 'Probably
not.'

Maybe he is right in this earthly kingdom, where people live strictly on the external plane. Happiness is equated with good looks, relationships with important people, the right job and a fat bank account. Life devoid of these 'benefits' is too often equated with hopelessness.

What about life in God's kingdom? The success-equals-happiness and failure-equals-hopelessness equations don't exist. Everyone has exactly the same opportunity for a meaningful life. Why? Because whole-ness and meaning in life are not the products of what you have or don't have, what you've done or haven't done. You are already a whole person and possess a life of infinite meaning and purpose because of who you are – a child of God. The only identity equation that works in God's kingdom is you plus Christ equals wholeness and meaning.

If our relationship with God is the key to wholeness, why do so many believers struggle with their identity, security, significance, sense of worth and spiritual matu-rity? Ignorance is probably the primary reason. The prophet Hosea said, 'My people are destroyed for lack of knowledge' (4:6). For others it is carnality, the lack of repentance and faith in God, and some are being deceived by the father of lies. This deception was brought home to me a few years ago when I was counseling a Christian girl who was the victim of satanic oppression.

I asked her, 'Who are you?'

'I'm evil,' she answered.

'You're not evil. How can a child of God be evil? Is that how you see yourself?' She nodded.

Now she may have done some evil things, but at the core of her being she wasn't evil. This was evident by the deep remorse she felt after sinning. She was basing her identity on the wrong equation. She was letting Satan's accusations influence her perception of herself instead of believing the truth.

Sadly, a great number of Christians are trapped in the same downward spiral. We fail, so we see ourselves as failures, which only leads to more failure. We sin, so we see our selves as sinners, which only leads to more sin. We have been deceived into believing that what we do determines who we are. That false belief sends us into a tailspin of hopelessness and more defeat. On the other hand, 'The Spirit Himself bears witness with our spirit that we are children of God' (Rom. 8:16). God wants us to know who we are so we can start living accordingly. Being a child of God who is alive and free in Christ should determine what we do. Then we are working *out* our salvation (see Phil. 2:12), not for our salvation.

Hand of God

Alistair Begg

Are we hapless victims of life's whims? Driven by some blind force?

A thousand times, 'No!' says Alistair Begg. Instead, he says it's a comforting fact that 'God rules and overrules in the circumstances of life'.

From his trademark fresh and enlightening perspective, Alistair Begg shows how God's providential hand was at work in the twists and turns of the life of Joseph the patriarch and how God works similarly today in the lives of His people.

Here is a narrative account of how God transforms overwhelming tragedy into unsurpassed triumph.

Alistair Begg is a pastor, broadcaster and author.

Moody Press
ISBN: 0-80241-703-5
(hardback)

Price: £12.99

£9.99 with money off voucher

Chapter 1

Family Ties

We know that in all things God works for the good of those who love him, who have been called according to his purpose."

Those who have been Christians for any length of time, may find that the page in their Bible which contains Romans 8:28 may be a little worn, even smudged. And with good reason. This great verse is a promise from God that we are not hapless victims of life, at the mercy of fate or chance. We are not driven along by some blind, impersonal force.

On the contrary, we are the objects of God's providential care. We are under His guiding and protecting hand.

The providence of God is "that continued exercise of the divine energy whereby the creator preserves all his creatures, is operative in all that comes to pass in the world, and directs all things to their appointed end" (Berkhof).

The implications of this truth are staggering because they impact every area and every moment of our lives. This truth is one of the things that separates believers from unbelievers. We need not be concerned about Sagittarius or Gemini or the other signs of the zodiac, or about the movements of the planets and other silly things that preoccupy pagan minds. Jesus says they may run after these things (Matthew 6:32), but as His people we are to be different.

So we are faced with this incredible truth that God rules and overrules in all the circumstances of life. Romans 8:28 is not a pious platitude to be mumbled at a bedside or a graveside when we don't know what else to say but want to be helpful. It is truth that's meant for life, so what we need is a real-life illustration of how this truth looks "with skin on."

That's what we hope to discover in this book. This biblical doctrine is classically expressed in the story of Joseph. As we trace the powerful principle of God's providential care unfolding in the life of the patriarch Joseph, we will find that his story is probably *the* classic Old Testament illustration of Romans 8:28 in action.

If you enjoy stories as much as I do, I can assure you that we are at the threshold of a classic in the story of Joseph. In deed, it is an epic, a saga. The biography of Joseph covers more space than that given to any of the other heroes in the book of Genesis. That's amazing when you realize that this group includes Abraham, the friend of God and the father of all who believe.

Even people who have only a scant knowledge of the Old Testament probably know of Joseph for the same reason many people know of Noah and the ark or Jonah and the great fish. His story is memorialized by something visually unusual – his multicolored coat.

And for those who have no biblical clue at all, Joseph may still be a familiar name, courtesy of the popular Broadway musical *Joseph and the Amazing Technicolor Dreamcoat,* by Timothy Rice and Andrew Lloyd-Weber. Joseph, as we are about to discover, is a man worth knowing.

Joseph's birth is recorded in Genesis 30:23–24, and he is mentioned several times in subsequent chapters. But we are introduced to him in depth when he is seventeen years old, a young man tending the flocks of his father, Jacob, with his brothers (Genesis 37:2). Between this notice and the record of Joseph's death ninety-three years later at the age of 110 (50:26), we have the details of a truly amazing life presented to us in biblical Technicolor.

The story of Joseph is a tale of jealousy, deceit, slavery, misrepresentation, injustice, lust, rivalry, and forgiveness. It pits brother against brother. We encounter imprisonment and deep trials that do not produce self-pity, and prosperity that does not bring the accompanying pride.

Joseph's life encompasses all of this and more. And in it all the overarching theme is that of the sovereign hand of God manifesting itself in His providential care over His dearly loved children and bringing about all that He has purposed in the affairs of time.

Joseph's life ought to be for us a story of great encouragement and reassurance as we make our way in the walk of faith, carrying with us the baggage of our past, the fears of our present, and the prospects of our future. We are sometimes tempted to wonder in the midst of all the pieces of the jigsaw puzzle of life, *Does God care? Is God in control? And if so, what might we expect?*

We don't know if Joseph asked those questions before he was seventeen. We will see that his early life did include a great amount of turmoil, in large part because his father, Jacob's, past was catching up with him.

But if Joseph never had reason to wonder what God was doing in his life, all of that changed when he turned seventeen. Before we look at the events that sent Joseph's life spinning, let's consider the influences on his life up to that point.

Joseph's Background

Where did Joseph come from? If you were to encounter his name for the first time in Genesis 3 7:2, you might ask this. Did Joseph have the kind of family background we might expect to produce a person of such exceptional character?

What were Joseph's family ties? All of us have them, and they all mean something. Our family ties can be frustrating and full, blessed and benighted.

There's no question that Joseph came from quite a family. No other seventeen-year-old can boast that his great-grandfather is Abraham; his grandfather, Isaac; and his father, Jacob. By looking at Jacob we can trace the family ties and the influences of Joseph's early life.

Jacob's Early Life

Jacob's character was revealed at his birth when he grasped the heel of his twin Esau and was given a name that means "deceiver" or "chiseler" (see Genesis 25:26, margin). Jacob was aptly named for he was skillful at manipulating people and events to get things to turn out the way he wanted. The first thing we learn about him is that he chiseled his elder brother, Esau, out of his birthright (vv. 27–34).

Then, as recorded in Genesis 27, Jacob deceived his father Isaac into conferring upon him the blessing that should have belonged to Esau. When Esau found out, he said, "Isn't he rightly named Jacob? He has deceived me these two times" (27:36). Esau vowed to kill Jacob, so his mother Rebekah sent Jacob to live with her brother Laban in the land of Paddan Aram (2 8:2).

It was there that Jacob met and fell in love with Rachel, the younger daughter of Laban (29:9–10, 16–18). Jacob loved Rachel so passionately he offered to work for his Uncle Laban seven years for Rachel's hand in marriage.

Now, ironically, Uncle Laban was a bit of a schemer himself. So when the seven years were completed and Jacob said to Laban, "Give me my wife. My time is completed, and I want to lie with her" (v. 2 1), Laban deceived Jacob by slipping his older daughter Leah into the wedding chamber.

It sounds like a soap opera, doesn't it? You know that when Laban went to bed that night, he must have said to his wife, "Wait until Jacob discovers what I've done. It is going to be unbelievable."

When Jacob realized he had been deceived, Laban tried to legitimize the whole affair by saying it was the custom that he couldn't give away his younger daughter until he had given away his older daughter.

But Laban had another deal for Jacob. "Finish [Leah's] bridal week; then we will give you [Rachel] also, in return for another seven years of work" (v. 27). Such was Jacob's passionate love for Rachel that he said, "Fine, it's a deal." So Jacob married Rachel too.

Joseph's Family

With Jacob's marriages, the family album of Joseph began to fill up. The dining room was regularly in need of extra chairs. Jacob favoured Rachel, but God closed her womb and opened the womb of Leah. God is sovereign in the details of life.

In rapid succession the Bible describes how the first twelve children of Jacob were born – eleven sons and a daughter. Altogether, Leah bore Jacob six sons and the only daughter, Dinah. Leah also gave her maidservant Zilpah to Jacob, and through her Jacob had two more sons.

When Rachel could not conceive, she gave *her* maidservant Bilhah to Jacob, and Bilhah bore two sons. Finally, in Genesis 30:22–24 we read, "God remembered Rachel … and opened her womb. She became pregnant and gave birth to a son…. She named him Joseph."

This was quite a family! One father, four mothers, two who were wives and two who were concubines, eleven sons, and one daughter. And at the end of this mixed-up, complicated family Joseph arrived, for the present the youngest of Jacob's sons. (Benjamin would not be born for several years, and in giving birth to him, Rachel would die [35:16–18]).

Between Joseph's birth and his appearance on the scene for good in Genesis 37:2 his name appears only three times, and in each of those he is given the barest mention (33:2, 7; 35:24). But he was part of the family during the events recorded in Genesis 31–36, which cover the first seventeen years of his life.

Joseph's Formative Years

These were Joseph's formative years, a part of God's providential work to mold him for the future God had for him. God was already forming Joseph's character for an exceptional, sovereign purpose that neither he nor any of the others in his family would understand for many years.

So by way of summary, let's look at what happened to this lad and his family during the years between his birth and the real beginning of his story. What a record it is.

The Family's Flight from Laban

Sometime after Joseph was born, Jacob decided it was time to go back home and face his brother Esau in Canaan. We don't know how old Joseph was at this time – maybe six or seven years old. If so, he was old enough to take in his father's announcement across the dinner table, "We're moving back to Canaan."

Joseph probably didn't understand what it all meant, but he would have known that a big change was under way. One of his earliest recollections as a child must have been the hurried flight from the home of his grandfather Laban as Jacob took his family and flocks and left by night without Laban's knowledge (3 1: 1 7–21).

I remember all the questions from the children when our family moved from Scotland to the United States. "When are we going? How are we going to get there? What will we do when we get there?"

When we arrived in the United States, the children didn't know where they were. When we went on vacation, they thought they were going home. They just couldn't process all the information involved in a big move like that. Their tiny lives were in an amazing whirl.

The experience of his family's flight to Canaan would have been much the same for Joseph. The family left under the cover of darkness so they wouldn't be detected. Jacob knew that if Laban found out they were leaving, he would try to stop them. And so in the moonlight little Joseph was put on a camel with his mother, and the large caravan started out toward Canaan.

I can hear Joseph asking Jacob, "Father, why are we running away at night? Don't you like Grandfather? Doesn't Grandfather love us? Shouldn't we say good-bye to him?"

And then days later, when Laban caught up with the family (vv. 22–23), I wonder if Joseph was standing on the fringe listening as his grandfather looked at his father and said:

> "What have you done? You've deceived me, and you've car-
> ried off my daughters like captives in war. Why did you run off
> secretly and deceive me? Why didn't you tell me, so I could
> send you away with joy and singing to the music of tambou-
> rines and harps? You didn't even let me kiss my grandchildren
> and my daughters good-by. You have done a foolish thing."
> (vv. 26–2 8)

Now I don't know about your relationship with your grand father, but my grandpa and I were as close as we could be. He never drove a car, as a result of wounds he had suffered in the First World War, and so we became experts in public transport in Glasgow. I've been on just about every bus to every terminus in the system.

I would ride the buses with my grandpa just to go places with him. At other times Grandpa and I would ride the whole subway system maybe three times, going nowhere, just me sit ting beside him, listening to his stories. So I wouldn't want any body tearing me away from my grandpa without the chance to kiss him good-bye.

But that's what happened to Joseph. He was going to have a lot of tearing away in his life – many times when he didn't get to say good-bye. He was going to have to learn how to weep and how to deal with pain. And even in these early life circumstances, God was forming Joseph in prepa-ration for what was to come.

The final scene in Genesis 31 is one we need to etch onto our memories as far as the life of Joseph is concerned.

Jacob and Laban made a covenant together then had a meal to seal the agreement, and Laban spent the night before going back home (vv. 43–54).

I want you to sense the emotion here. If you have ever moved a great distance from home, you know this "night before" experience well. The family is gathered, and there is a great reunion. But the joy is clouded by the prospect of the next morning and the separation.

So it was in Joseph's family. The text tells us, "Early the next morning Laban kissed his grandchildren and his daughters and blessed them. Then he left and returned home" (v. 55). Don't you think Laban squeezed those boys, maybe giving little Joseph an extra hug as the baby of the clan?

The Meeting with Esau

That part of the story comes to an end without any arguments or ugly scenes, but Jacob's distress was just beginning. Now he had to face the dreaded prospect of meeting his brother, Esau, who was coming to meet him with four hundred men. Fear gripped Jacob's heart at the very thought (32:7).

Again, Joseph would have been in on this to some degree. He may not have grasped the whole picture, but he knew something was wrong. He knew his father was afraid. Maybe he heard Jacob and Rachel talking in the tent, the way my mom and dad used to talk as they did the dishes. I would listen from the doorway, and I knew when my dad was troubled. And that is an apt word to describe Jacob's state in a very personal encounter with God.

You'll remember that Jacob divided his family and possessions and sent them on ahead. Separated from his

family and his possessions, he encountered God in a surprising, personal, necessary way, and the result was permanent. He received a new name and a whole new
identity.

In the morning, when Jacob returned to his family, he
was limping as a result of his wrestling match with the
Angel of the Lord. I don't know if he ever told Joseph what
had happened that night, but the event had clearly stamped
Jacob, for when the family got to Shechem, Jacob (now
called Israel) built an altar to the Lord to set his family apart
from the surrounding culture (33:18–20).

The Tragedy at Shechem

We are sketching in large strokes the background scenes of
Joseph's life from birth to the age of seventeen, when his
story begins in earnest. Joseph's father, Jacob (later called
Israel), was reconciled to his brother, Esau, but when the
family camped at Shechem, a dreadful tale unfolded –
Dinah was raped by a young man also named Shechem,
and Simeon and Levi devised a fearful reprisal against the
men of the city (34:1–31).

Joseph may have been eleven or twelve at this time, and
we can imagine what went through his mind as he heard all
the hushed conversations and the extreme agitation of his
older brothers. In it all God was working to form the character of this lad.

From Shechem the clan moved on under God's
orders to Bethel, where Jacob had stopped on his flight
from Esau (35:1; cf. 28:10–22). Jacob built an altar there
to purify his household, and then bereavement touched
his home.

The Death of Rachel

First, a woman named Deborah, the nurse to Jacob's mother, Rebekah, died and was mourned (35:8). Then Jacob suffered the loss of his beloved wife Rachel as she was giving birth to Benjamin (v. 18).

The birth of Benjamin was a key moment in Joseph's life. As the next youngest, Joseph would have had the closest emotional ties to Benjamin. Besides this, they were the only sons of Rachel. But the day of Benjamin's birth was one during which joy and sorrow mingled as life had ebbed from Joseph's mother in her final pangs of childbirth.

So once again the threads of pain and sorrow and bereavement were woven into Joseph's life. Then he had to deal with the death of his grandfather, Isaac (35:29). Another funeral, another reminder of the frailty of life, the reality of death, and the necessity of faith.

The Grace of God

There is much more in these chapters that will reward your careful study. When we arrive at chapter 37, the camera lens is focused upon Joseph as the central person in the narrative. Now we are ready to look into the eyes of a young man of seventeen who has already been through more excitement and intrigue and trauma than most of us will experience in a lifetime.

In modern-day terms, Joseph came from a dysfunctional family. Indeed, we all came from a dysfunctional background because sin makes people dysfunctional. But when you take all the sins of a large number of selfish people and mix them together in a family, you have an

entity badly out of alignment with wheels turning in different directions.

We can summarize this background briefly. We need to
remember that in the rough-and-tumble of a
less-than-perfect family life, God was preparing Joseph for
the role He had planned for him. As a matter of fact, the
only explanation for the life of Joseph and the role he
played is found in the electing grace of God. There is no
human reason whatsoever that Joseph should have
emerged from the emotional and spiritual carnage of his
family life to be the incredible man of God he was. The
only way we can explain it is to say God purposed that it
should be so. "God moves in a mysterious way, His
wonders to perform. He plants His footsteps in the sea and
rides upon the storm."

We mustn't allow our circumstances and disappoint-
ments to become the excuse for the choices we make in
life. God is greater than all of that, and He can bring beauty
out of ashes. Our trials come, Augustine said, "to prove us
and to improve us." The mosaic of Joseph's background
also provides us with a striking reminder of the impact a
father's life has on his children.

Jacob was not a good model of integrity. He did poorly
when it came to decisiveness. He was slow when it came to
action. He tended to avoid issues rather than face them. But
God chose to use this imperfect father to raise the boy He
had chosen to redeem His people from famine through his
experiences in Egypt.

What of us parents? What is the legacy we are leaving?
What stories will our children tell? When they stand and
gaze at our tombstone, what then? Be encouraged that out
of the chaos of Joseph's background came a man God used
as a stirring example of His grace.

Dear Paul

Bridget Plass

What if it were possible to ask the apostle Paul all the questions we would like to ask and to challenge him on his more controversial statements. What might he have to say to us?

Bridget Plass uses the concept of imagined correspondence between Paul and a widely varying group of contemporary men and women to explore the apostle's teaching. Career woman, defeated housewife, 'disgusted' from Brixham – each fictional correspondent has problems and opinions. Each is answered 'by Paul' with Bridget's usual blend of insight, fact and humour.

Bridget Plass is an accomplished speaker, author and contributor to BRF/Christian Press' 'Day by Day with God'.

The Bible Reading Fellowship
ISBN: 1-84101-038-3

Price: £5.99

£4.99 with money off voucher

Introduction

Before you read this book, I want to point out one or two
simple facts to those of you who might struggle with the
concept of a correspondence taking place between Paul
and a group of 21st-century men and women. To start
with, this book is fictional. Admittedly all Paul's 'replies' are
based as closely as I could manage on facts drawn from Acts
and from his letters, but it is indisputably a work of fiction.
Of course it is not possible for such a correspondence to
take place. Neither does it imply that I believe in contact-
ing the saints. It is quite simply a case of *'What if...?'*

What if it were possible to ask Paul all the questions we
would like to ask and to challenge him on his more controversial statements. What might he have to say to us? I don't
know how he would choose to reply if we wrote to him,
but trying to guess has been great fun. I hope my guesses
might prove helpful to those of you who have struggled to
reconcile some of Paul's most famous declarations with
some of his most dogmatic. You may, of course, totally dis-
agree with the replies I credit to Paul: 'He'd never have said
that!' If so, try writing your own. Or use the letters from
Madge and co. as discussion starting points on how you
think Paul would have responded.

Let me share with you a couple of typical reactions I have encountered when telling friends what I am trying to do. The first is from my male friends. Do you know, I hadn't realized that the cerebral understanding of Pauline thought has been considered such a male prerogative until I registered the surprise and, dare I say, kindly doubt in their eyes! The second is from some of my female friends who have expressed their disgust that Paul, whom they consider a priggish, narrow-minded little misogynist, should receive such intense focus from a woman!

So why did I want to try to discover what Paul might have to say to individuals struggling with the pressures of a post-modem world? First, because there is no other figure in the Bible who has produced such a passionate response in me. I passionately love, hate, respect and despise the things he has written.

The second is that I confess I am ashamed at the way that many women of today dismiss what Paul has to say on the role of women within marriage and the Church, without really giving him the benefit of the doubt. I consider us worthy of more than that. Whether we like to admit it or not, we are rather in his debt. God himself chose Paul to bring the good news to us, the Gentiles. The word Ananias uses when he tells Paul that he has been singled out for this immense task is the same verb, *eklegomia,* that is used in Luke's Gospel when Jesus chooses his twelve apostles. Not only that, but Jesus himself appeared to Paul, thus adding further proof that Paul was uniquely qualified to bear witness. After his resurrection, Jesus appeared to all his apostles, making it clear beyond any shadow of doubt that he was alive. On the road to Damascus he added Paul to the Twelve.

Lastly, God filled Paul with the power of the Holy Spirit, anointing his ministry and allowing him to preach repentance and forgiveness. Paul is the most famous anointed evangelist of all time. The churches he planted planted ours. The words that he wrote and spoke laid the foundations of church practice and doctrine from then to now (quite apart from popping up at every wedding and funeral I have ever been to!) And whatever we may think of some of what he said, he lived out his calling through every hardship imaginable, including shipwrecks, beatings, illness, loneliness and imprisonment. Let's face it, he is no lightweight to be tossed out of our spiritual ring!

So I invite you to join me in the company of this controversial man of God. Just how familiar are we with everything Paul wrote? How much do we know about the cultural context in which he operated? This book aims to catch a glimpse, not only of the passion that drove him on, but also of the compassion he had for those little churches that he founded and the individuals who were involved with them. Perhaps we will come to understand a little better why his 'dear friend the doctor' Luke liked and respected him so much, and why Timothy remained close to him throughout his ministry and appeared to love him dearly. We may even stop seeing him as a single-issue fanatic, and indeed start to question whether our obsession with the comparatively few remarks he made about women makes us just as intolerant as he seems to be.

Beverley

Dear Paul,

I am really at a loss to understand what all this hoo-ha is about being able to write to you, and I feel I want to challenge your audacity in presuming you have anything to say to the world I inhabit.

My father attended our local Anglican church and always claimed that his faith gave meaning to his life. I have no problem with that if it made him happy. I loved him very much and was quite content to go along with him to his church on high days and holidays. He and I even had infrequent but extremely lively and rather enjoyable discussions on the subject of Christianity before he died. I consider myself fortunate to have had a father who appreciated my independence and freedom of thought. He never pressurized me into believing or made me feel in any way guilty. I can still see his gentle smile and arms-up surrender when I beat him in argument. He used to take his revenge during the game of draughts with which we would often conclude our evenings together. I miss it all, but I have to say that I never heard anything to make me see the relevance of either Jesus Christ or indeed your good self to my life.

Look at it from my point of view. I am 23 years old, female and unmarried. I have a degree in Communications, I work as a PA in a small but successful modelling agency I already earn a far better salary than my father ever did, I have my own car, my own flat and above all my independence. I awake in the morning to my radio alarm, use my remote control to turn on my television, and listen to an up-to-date news report of exactly what is happening throughout the world. I check my mailbag on my computer and my fax machine for messages. On the basis of these I make phone calls on my mobile phone, arrange my boss's day (incidentally, a woman aged 30), might well have a phone conference, and also pay any urgent bills using my credit card. And that is just in the first half-an-hour of my day!

Be honest, Paul, what do you see when you look at our world? Are you not amazed at our progress, our scientific advances, our sophistication? Do you not marvel at what men and women have achieved in the last one hundred years, since religion has ceased to be used by so many as a prop and an easy answer to all mysteries? This is possible because we have decided to take control of our environment. Do you ever wonder what you might have done or said had you been born two thousand years later? Would you still be offering the same advice? Selling the same line? My father trusted you, Sir, so please don't let him down by replying untruthfully.

I await your reply with considerable interest.
Yours sincerely,

B.R. Palmer

Dear B.R. Palmer,

Your letter interests me greatly. Reading between the lines,
I suspect your delightful father lacked a certain amount of
ambition, unlike yourself. You obviously loved him a great
deal and miss his company. You also miss his admiration
and concern and, dare I suggest, the 'lively discussions' you
had about his religion. I believe I have been called the father of modern Christianity and have even been a father
figure to one or two of my young evangelists, but the role
of surrogate father you are unconsciously offering me is a
new one.

Point number one – I was not unambitious. Indeed, as a
young student studying under one of the leading rabbinic
teachers of the known world, I was tipped for the top,
groomed for a place on the governing body called the Sanhedrin. Neither, my dear young lady friend, was I to be
found dressed in an AD50 equivalent of a fawn coloured
knitted cardigan. Do you know anything at all about
Tarsus, the place where I grew up? We may not have
invented the microchip but we were a pretty sophisticated
bunch. Apart from having a university for Stoic studies,
Tarsus was considered to be the centre of Greek culture,
with a flourishing theatre and sports stadium.

But then, I wouldn't dream of insulting your obvious
intelligence by reminding you of the extraordinarily sophisticated lifestyle of both the Greeks and the Romans. I expect
you are quite warm in the morning while you make all those
important phone calls. Did you enjoy a pleasant hot shower
after all that strenuous phoning? Central heating? Any idea
who invented it? Oh yes, of course…

So, having got some of the rather slim insults out of the
way, let's look more closely at the rest of your letter. What

else do our world and yours have in common? You mention the fact that you hear news from all over the world, just as it happens. But does it really happen exactly as you hear it? I believe you have a somewhat dubious newspaper entitled the *News of the World*. Does that say it all? Is it not still the case that political gain, economic interest and individual bias still play a part in determining how much truth you actually receive? Is it not the case that undercover bribery is as prevalent in your world as it was in ours, when Caiphas and the Sanhedrin, motivated purely by self-interest, set out to murder Jesus Christ?

You say you have a degree in Communications. Presumably, then, you have studied the effect of the subtle propaganda machinery employed to a greater or lesser extent by every government in the world since civilization began, sometimes to truly devilish ends.

Are there really no Herods in the 21st century? No leaders pre pared to sacrifice the lives of innocents to further the safety, wealth and stature of their personal dynasty? Surely, Ms Palmer, you are not so naïve and unsophisticated as to believe that human nature has progressed? Has illness been eradicated, poverty erased, prejudice purified? Has education for all brought equality? Has liberation brought peace? Is there no loneliness or fear? No evil? No hypocrisy? No brutality?

I cannot comment on your world. I can only instruct from mine, but I am confident that whatever may have changed in the world, the human heart with its capacity to deceive and to be deceived, to corrupt and to be corrupted, has not changed. Neither, I am quite sure, have the eternal hopes and yearnings for personal peace. In AD57, approximately one thousand nine hundred and seventy-eight years before you were born, I was closely involved with the

newly planted church in Rome. Even you will have difficulty equating your image of dressing-gowned dodderers
with anything you have ever heard of life in Rome! As a
society they knew everything there was to know about
refinement and decadence but also about excellence. They
would have understood ambition! Incidentally, did you
know it was possible even for a slave to reach a position of
influence in the city?

So what was I doing? What was I offering them? You
talk about the prop of religion. You say it was used as a sim-
plistic solution to the mysteries of the universe, and, of
course, there is truth in that. There has always been a desire
to understand the world. The Romans I was writing to
had, as you know, many gods to whom they prayed.

Presumably, you think I was a sort of door-to-door
salesman, offering what I had been convinced was a more
up-to-date product – a belief system which may have
seemed radical at the time, and able to answer questions
more thoroughly, but which, in the 21st century, is clearly
redundant and rather charmingly old-fashioned. Obviously, you will be expecting me to defend what I did, especially as my way of life involved such high personal risk.

Certainly I do want to say that the job given to me was
extremely difficult and nothing like as cosy as you have
suggested. It took every bit of my ingenuity and a few
out-and-out miracles to get me safely into as many influ-
ential situations as possible, but when I got there my
message was always the same. Again and again I tried to
point out that it is in the glorious mystery of the created
world that God's glory, his eternal power and divine nature
can be seen—and that when people stop glorifying God
the Creator and, in their foolishness, start to worship
created things, society becomes so decadent that even

children are not safe. You may not have exchanged the glory of an immortal God for images made to look like men and reptiles and animals and birds, but you do seem to have created your own gods, called Computer, Car and even, laughingly, Household Appliance. To me, Jesus was not a take-or-leave alternative to Apollo or Zeus. Nor is he now an alternative to a no-bag vacuum cleaner! I was not offering a free sample of the Holy Spirit with every contract signed. To me it was a matter of life and death whether those who heard my story believed it or not. Jesus was and is the Son of the living God. Only through accepting this by an act of faith and obedience can one become whole and healed and truly alive.

Much as I admire your delightful parent, I cannot condone his *laissez-faire* attitude to your energetically determined lack of belief. Neither do I see your enjoyable arguments about religion as an alternative intelligence test to a game of draughts. It is true that I thought the world as we know it was intended by God to come to an end during my lifetime, and this fuelled my determination to stress the urgency of the need to accept Jesus as the only possible salvation. Such a level of passion didn't leave much room for lighthearted ness. Also, I can see why you find the things I stand for such an anachronism. After all, your society is still recovering from a rather disgusting preoccupation with hell that you inherited from the century before. Glancing over the last two thousand years, I have to tell you that I expect to see a massive swing back. That is, if your society has sorted out a more effective way of dealing with spiralling decadence than either Greece or Rome managed! Or unless God decides enough is enough!

Ms Palmer, I refuse to smile at you or to raise my hands in defeat, or to play draughts. The continuation of our discussion is too urgently important to me and, I might add, to your father. Will you pick up the gauntlet I have thrown down? I have all the time in eternity to fight you for your life. It's up to you.

Yours,

Paul

Holy Bible – Living Water

New Living Translation

Have you ever longed to read the Bible in the language we speak today? To discover a translation that conveys God's eternal truth in a way that is relevant in the 21st century?

The New Living Translation is both readable and reliable. Its clear, accessible style makes reading the Bible incredibly refreshing. And the newly launched Living Water edition brings the added benefit of British spellings, style and vocabulary, including metric weights and measurements – making the New Living Translation even more relevant for today.

Tyndale House Publishers
ISBN: 0-84234-027-0
(hardback)

Price: £14.99

£8.99 with money off voucher

New Testament

Matthew

Author: Matthew (Levi)
Date: A.D. 60–65
Genre: Gospel
Summary: This Gospel was written with the Jew in mind and therefore has many references to Old Testament prophecies that were fulfilled by Jesus. It contains at least 129 quotations or allusions to the Old Testament. Matthew's objective was to show the Jewish people that Jesus was indeed their long-awaited Messiah.

Sermon on the Mount

5 One day as the crowds were gathering, Jesus went up the mountainside with his disciples and sat down to teach them.

The Beatitudes

² This is what he taught them:

³ 'God blesses those who realize their need for him,'
      for the Kingdom of Heaven is given to them.
⁴ God blesses those who mourn,
      for they will be comforted.
⁵ God blesses those who are gentle and lowly,
      for the whole earth will belong to them.
⁶ God blesses those who are hungry and thirsty for justice,
      for they will receive it in full.
⁷ God blesses those who are merciful,
      for they will be shown mercy.
⁸ God blesses those whose hearts are pure,
      for they will see God.
⁹ God blesses those who work for peace,
      for they will be called the children of God.
¹⁰ God blesses those who are persecuted
            because they live for God,
      for the Kingdom of Heaven is theirs.

¹¹ "God blesses you when you are mocked and persecuted and lied about because you are my followers. ¹² Be happy about it! Be very glad! For a great reward awaits you

---

5:3 Greek *the poor in spirit.*

in heaven. And remember, the ancient prophets were persecuted, too.

Teaching about Salt and Light

[13] "You are the salt of the earth. But what good is salt if it has lost its flavour! Can you make it useful again? It will be thrown out and trampled underfoot as worthless. [14] You are the light of the world – like a city on a mountain, glowing in the night for all to see. [15] Don't hide your light under a basket! Instead, put it on a stand and let it shine for all. [16] In the same way, let your good deeds shine out for all to see, so that everyone will praise your heavenly Father.

Teaching about the Law

[17] "Don't misunderstand why I have come. I did not come to abolish the law of Moses or the writings of the prophets. No, I came to fulfil them. [18] I assure you, until heaven and earth disappear even the smallest detail of God's law will remain until its purpose is achieved. [19] So if you break the smallest commandment and teach others to do the same, you will be the least in the Kingdom of Heaven. But anyone who obeys God's laws and teaches them will be great in the Kingdom of Heaven.

[20] "But I warn you – unless you obey God better than the teachers of religious law and the Pharisees do, you can't enter the Kingdom of Heaven at all!

Teaching about Anger

[21] "You have heard that the law of Moses says, 'Do not murder. If you commit murder, you are subject to judge-

ment.'★ [22] But I say if you are angry with someone, ★ you are subject to judgement! If you call someone an idiot★ you are in danger of being brought before the high council. And if you curse someone, ★ you are in danger of the fires of hell.

[23] "So if you are standing before the altar in the Temple, offering a sacrifice to God, and you suddenly remember that someone has something against you, [24] leave your sacrifice there beside the altar. Go and be reconciled to that person. Then come and offer your sacrifice to God. [25] Come to terms quickly with your enemy before it is too late and you are dragged into court, handed over to an officer, and thrown in jail. [26] I assure you that you won't be free again until you have paid the last penny.

Teaching about Adultery

[27] "You have heard that the law of Moses says, 'Do not commit adultery.'★ [28] But I say, anyone who even looks at a woman with lust in his eye has already committed adultery with her in his heart. [29] So if your eye – even if it is your good eye★ – causes you to lust, gouge it out and throw it away. It is better for you to lose one part of your body than for your whole body to be thrown into hell. [30] And if your hand – even if it is your stronger hand★ – causes you to sin, cut it off and throw it away. It is better for you to lose one part of your body than for your whole body to be thrown into hell.

5:21 Exod 20:13; Deut 5:17. 5:22a Greek *your brother;* also in 5:23. Some manuscripts add *without cause.* 5:22b Greek uses an Aramaic term of contempt: *If you say to your brother, "Raca".* 5:22c Greek *if you say, "You fool".* 5:27 Exod 20:14; Deut 5:18. 5:29 Greek *your right eye.* 5:30 Greek *your right hand.*

Teaching about Divorce

[31] "You have heard that the law of Moses says, 'A man can divorce his wife by merely giving her a letter of divorce.'★ [32] But I say that a man who divorces his wife, unless she has been unfaithful, causes her to commit adultery. And anyone who marries a divorced woman commits adultery.

Teaching about Vows

[33] "Again, you have heard that the law of Moses says, 'Do not break your vows; you must carry out the vows you have made to the Lord.'★ [34] But I say, don't make any vows! If you say, 'By heaven!' it is a sacred vow because heaven is God's throne. [35] And if you say, 'By the earth!' it is a sacred vow because the earth is his footstool. And don't swear, 'By Jerusalem!' for Jerusalem is the city of the great King. [36] Don't even swear, 'By my head!' for you can't turn one hair white or black. [37] Just say a simple, 'Yes, I will,' or 'No, I won't.' Your word is enough. To strengthen your promise with a vow shows that something is wrong. ★

Teaching about Revenge

[38] "You have heard that the law of Moses says, 'If an eye is injured, injure the eye of the person who did it. If a tooth gets knocked out, knock out the tooth of the person who did it.'★ [39] But I say, don't resist an evil person! If you are slapped on the right cheek, turn the other, too. [40] If you are

5:31 Deut 24:1. 5:33 Num 30:2, 5.37 *Or Anything beyond this is from the evil one.* 5:38 Greek *"An eye for an eye and a tooth for a tooth".* Exod 21:24, Lev 24:20; Deut 19:21.

ordered to court and your shirt is taken from you, give your coat, too. [41] If a soldier demands that you carry his gear for a kilometre,⋆ carry it two kilometres. [42] Give to those who ask, and don't turn away from those who want to borrow.

Teaching about Love for Enemies

[43] "You have heard that the law of Moses says, 'Love your neighbour'⋆ and hate your enemy. [44] But I say, love your enemies! ⋆ Pray for those who persecute you! [45] In that way, you will be acting as true children of your Father in heaven. For he gives his sunlight to both the evil and the good, and he sends rain on the just and on the unjust, too. [46] If you love only those who love you, what good is that? Even corrupt tax collectors do that much. [47] If you are kind only to your friends,⋆ how are you different from anyone else? Even pagans do that. [48] But you are to be perfect, even as your Father in heaven is perfect.

Teaching about Giving to the Needy

6 "Take care! Don't do your good deeds publicly, to be admired, because then you will lose the reward from your Father in heaven. [2] When you give a gift to someone in need, don't shout about it as the hypocrites do – blowing trumpets in the synagogues and streets to call attention to their acts of charity! I assure you, they have received all the reward they will ever get. [3] But when you give to someone,

---

5:41 Greek *Million* (1.5 kilometres or 4,854 feet). 5:43 Lev 19:18. 5:44 Some manuscripts add *Bless those who curse you, do good to those who hate you.* 5:47 Greek *your brothers.*

don't tell your left hand what your right hand is doing. ⁴ Give your gifts in secret, and your Father, who knows all secrets, will reward you.

Teaching about Prayer and Fasting

⁵ "And now about prayer. When you pray, don't be like the hypocrites who love to pray publicly on street comers and in the synagogues where everyone can see them. I assure you, that is all the reward they will ever get. ⁶ But when you pray, go away by yourself, shut the door behind you, and pray to your Father secretly. Then your Father, who knows all secrets, will reward you.

⁷ "When you pray, don't babble on and on as people of other religions do. They think their prayers are answered only by repeating their words again and again. ⁸ Don't be like them, because your Father knows exactly what you need even before you ask him! ⁹ Pray like this:

Our Father in heaven,
      may your name be honoured.
¹⁰ May your Kingdom come soon.
   May your will be done here on earth,
      just as it is in heaven.
¹¹ Give us our food for today, ★
¹² and forgive us our sins
         just as we have forgiven those who
            have sinned against us.
¹³ And don't let us yield to temptation,
         but deliver us from the evil one. ★

6:11 Or *for tomorrow.* 6:13 Or *from evil.* Some manuscripts add *for yours is the kingdom and the power and the glory for ever. Amen.*

[14] "If you forgive those who sin against you, your heavenly Father will forgive you. [15] But if you refuse to forgive others, your Father will not forgive your sins.

[16] "And when you fast, don't make it obvious, as the hypocrites do, who try to look pale and dishevelled so people will admire them for their fasting. I assure you, that is the only reward they will ever get. [17] But when you fast, comb your hair and wash your face. [18] Then no one will suspect you are fasting, except your Father, who knows what you do in secret. And your Father, who knows all secrets, will reward you.

Teaching about Money and Possessions

[19] "Don't store up treasures here on earth, where they can be eaten by moths and get rusty, and where thieves break in and steal. [20] Store your treasures in heaven, where they will never become moth-eaten or rusty and where they will be safe from thieves. [21] Wherever your treasure is, there your heart and thoughts will also be.

[22] "Your eye is a lamp for your body. A pure eye lets sunshine into your soul. [23] But an evil eye shuts out the light and plunges you into darkness. If the light you think you have is really darkness, how deep that darkness will be!

[24] "No one can serve two masters. For you will hate one and love the other, or be devoted to one and despise the other. You cannot serve both God and money.

[25] "So I tell you, don't worry about everyday life – whether you have enough food, drink, and clothes. Doesn't life consist of more than food and clothing? [26] Look at the birds. They don't need to plant or harvest or put food in barns, for your heavenly Father feeds them.

And you are far more valuable to him than they are. [27] Can all your worries add a single moment to your life? Of course not.

[28] "And why worry about your clothes? Look at the lilies and how they grow. They don't work or make their clothing [29] yet Solomon in all his glory was not dressed as beautifully as they are. [30] And if God cares so wonderfully for flowers that are here today and gone tomorrow, won't he more surely care for you? You have so little faith!

[31] "So don't worry about having enough food or drink or clothing. [32] Why be like the pagans who are so deeply concerned about these things? Your heavenly Father already knows all your needs, [33] and he will give you all you need from day to day if you live for him and make the Kingdom of God your primary concern.

[34] "So don't worry about tomorrow, for tomorrow will bring its own worries. Today's trouble is enough for today.

Don't Condemn Others

7 "Stop judging others, and you will not be judged. [2] For others will treat you as you treat them.★ Whatever measure you use in judging others, it will be used to measure how you are judged. [3] And why worry about a speck in your friend's eye★ when you have a log in your own? [4] How can you think of saying 'Let me help you get rid of that speck in your eye,' when you can't see past the log in

---

7:2 Or *for God will treat you as you treat others;* Greek reads *for with the judgement you judge, you will be judged.* 7:3 Greek *your brother's eye;* also in 7.5.

your own eye? [5] Hypocrite! First get rid of the log from your own eye; then perhaps you will see well enough to deal with the speck in your friend's eye.

[6] "Don't give what is holy to unholy people.★ Don't give pearls to swine! They will trample the pearls, then turn and attack you.

Effective Prayer

[7] "Keep on asking and you will be given what you ask for. Keep on looking, and you will find. Keep on knocking and the door will be opened. [8] For everyone who asks, receives. Everyone who seeks, finds. And the door is opened to everyone who knocks. [9] You parents – if your children ask for a loaf of bread, do you give them a stone instead? [10] Or if they ask for a fish, do you give them a snake? Of course not! [11] If you sinful people know how to give good gifts to your children, how much more will your heavenly Father give good gifts to those who ask him.

The Golden Rule

[12] "Do for others what you would like them to do for you. This is a summary of all that is taught in the law and the prophets.

The Narrow Gate

[13] "You can enter God's Kingdom only through the narrow gate. The highway to hell★ is broad, and its gate is wide for the many who choose the easy way. [14] But the gateway

---

7:6 Greek *Don't give the sacred to dogs.* 7:13 Greek *The way that leads to destruction.*

to life is small, and the road is narrow, and only a few ever find it.

The Tree and Its Fruit

[15] "Beware of false prophets who come disguised as harmless sheep, but are really wolves that will tear you apart. [16] You can detect them by the way they act, just as you can identify a tree by its fruit. You don't pick grapes from thorn bushes, or figs from thistles. [17] A healthy tree produces good fruit, and an unhealthy tree produces bad fruit. [18] A good tree can't produce bad fruit, and a bad tree can't produce good fruit. [19] So every tree that does not produce good fruit is chopped down and thrown into the fire. [20] Yes, the way to identify a tree or a person is by the kind of fruit that is produced.

True Disciples

[21] "Not all people who sound religious are really godly. They may refer to me as 'Lord,' but they still won't enter the Kingdom of Heaven. The decisive issue is whether they obey my Father in heaven [22] On judgement day many will tell me, 'Lord, Lord, we prophesied in your name and cast out demons in your name and performed many miracles in your name.' [23] But I will reply, 'I never knew you. Go away; the things you did were unauthorized. ★'

Building on a Solid Foundation

[24] "Anyone who listens to my teaching and obeys me is wise,

---

7:23 Or *unlawful*.

like a person who builds a house on solid rock. [25] Though the rain comes in torrents and the floodwaters rise and the winds beat against that house, it won't collapse, because it is built on rock. [26] But anyone who hears my teaching and ignores it is foolish, like a person who builds a house on sand. [27] When the rains and floods come and the winds beat against that house, it will fall with a mighty crash."

[28] After Jesus finished speaking, the crowds were amazed at his teaching [29] for he taught as one who had real authority – quite unlike the teachers of religious law.

The Message of the Living God

Peter Lewis

The Bible Speaks Today series has three aims:
    To expound the biblical text with accuracy
    To relate it to contemporary life, and
    To be readable

    All three come together in this work centred on the doctrine of God, and concentrating on the first five books of the Old Testament.

    It is more expository than systematic theology usually is, following connected passages on a biblical theme rather than grouping texts and concepts under a prearranged scheme.

    'The ultimate purpose of theology', says author Peter Lewis, 'is to lead us to the feet of the living God.'

    Peter Lewis is a theologian, preacher and pastor.

Inter-Varsity Press
ISBN: 0-85111-509-8

Price: £9.99

£7.99 with money off voucher

Introduction:

How can we know God?

Woody Allen, in *Love and Death,* says at one point: 'If God would only speak to me – just once. If he would only cough. If I could just see a miracle. If I could see a burning bush or the seas part. Or my Uncle Sasha pick up the check.'

There, I think, you have the mixture of timeless longing and trendy cynicism which characterizes much of the Western mind-set and personality today. Allen wants God – but on his own terms. And God won't play. Allen wants God the conversationalist: 'If God would only speak to me – just once.' God has, in fact, given him a Bible recording 1,400 years of speech, but a cough for Woody outweighs a covenant with Abraham or even a Calvary for Christ.

He wants God the conjuror ('If I could just see a miracle') but gives no guarantees he'd do anything about it. He probably wants God the friend and God the therapist too, but all he has is human beings: commonplace, flawed, stubborn, exploitive. Like his Uncle Sasha, who always lets other people pick up the bill.

How then can we know God and how can we know that we know him, if not the Woody Allen way?

1. Points of contact

In his fine book on effective Christian apologetics, *Bridge-Building,* Alister McGrath writes:

> The first major insight encountered by the reader of Scripture is that God created the world. Is it therefore surprising that this creation should bear witness to him? Or that the height of his creation, human beings, should carry a recognisable imprint of his nature? And that this imprint might have considerable value as a starting point for apologetics? Paul believed passionately in the theological truth and apologetic importance of this insight (Romans 1–2).[1]

Here is a God–given starting point within the created order itself which can act as a trigger, stimulating people to ask questions about the meaning of life or the reality of God. Through the generosity of God we have been left with a latent memory of him which can discern what Peter Berger famously called 'signals of transcendence' within human life.

However, McGrath continues:

> Points of contact are not in themselves adequate to bring people into the kingdom of God. They are starting points for that goal. Nor are they adequate in themselves to bring people to a specifically *Christian* faith … The apologist must show that the Christian gospel is consistent with these points of contact. It is able to explain them – and more than that: it is able to deliver all that they promise, turning hints into reality.[2]

---

[1] Alister McGrath, *Bridge-Building* (IVP, 1992), p. 18.
[2] Ibid., p. 19.

Because of universal sin, the falleness of our race from God and the corruption of the natural order, these things do not give us a sufficient knowledge of God or put us right with God. 'Fallen human nature is obliged to reflect upon a fallen creation... Like a cracked mirror, or a misty window, it presents us with a distorted image.'[3] We find within ourselves and our history as a race all sorts of confused and conflicting knowledge and ideas about God. We have a deep dissatisfaction with life without God, and yet are runaways from him. As Augustine famously said, 'You have made us for yourself, and our hearts are restless until they rest in you.' McGrath comments:

> The doctrines of creation and redemption combine to interpret this sense of dissatisfaction and lack of fulfilment as a loss of fellowship with God which can be restored. Augustine captured this idea perfectly when he spoke of a 'loving memory' of God. It is a *memory* of God, in that it is grounded in the doctrines of creation and redemption, which affirm that we have partially *lost* something through sin – and are somehow made aware of that loss through God's grace. It is a *loving* memory, in that it is experienced as a sense of divine nostalgia, of spiritual wistfulness. There is a thirst to have more of that which we already have only in part.[4]

Yet there is not only desire for God but also an antipathy for God in fallen, rebellious, human nature.[5] Paul says, 'The sinful mind is hostile to God. It does not submit to God's law, nor can it do so.'[6]

---

[3] Ibid., p . 23.
[4] Ibid., p. 21.
[5] Rom. 1:18.
[6] Rom. 8:7.

There is an ignorance of God which is 'due to the hardening of their hearts'.[7] Sin has made us allergic to holiness and guilt has made us liable to punishment.[8] Therefore we are in flight from 'home' as well as nostalgic for it. Sin has broken the relationship which marked us out as such a special creation. Now, as a race, we stand in proud independence, and in profound ambivalence about the knowledge of God. We want this knowledge – up to a point, and we don't want it to control our lives. This ambivalence has to be faced and dealt with. God's grace helps us to do that. This is the grace that is alone sufficient to arrest us in our flight, to bring us to our knees, to begin the conversation *with* our Maker (and not just conversations with others about him), to make us seek to know God by his own light and not just by our own. Such a dependence on grace is the true starting point in any journey to God.

2. Knowing God

John Calvin does not begin his *Institutes* by speaking of the 'existence' of God, but of the 'knowledge' of him.[9] He doesn't begin by asking 'Does God exist?' but 'How can God be known?' Calvin insists that we know God only because he lets himself be known and, furthermore, that we know him properly only from within a relationship of humility, worship and love.[10]

---

[7] Eph. 4:18.
[8] Rom. 2:1–5.
[9] Calvin *(Institutes)*, I. i.1.
[10] Ibid., I.i–ii.

Calvin's point is twofold. First, God must be known in his nature and character more than in terms of his essence. God's essence is largely beyond our knowing and it is enough for us to worship him in his immensity and his spirituality without presuming to go into matters infinitely beyond us. The question is not 'What is God?' but 'What am I meant to know of him which is proper to his glory?' Secondly, 'It is a favourite emphasis in Calvin that *pietas,* piety, in which reverence and love of God are joined, is prerequisite to any true knowledge of God.'[11] The knowledge of God must be personal, penitential and devout. In a word, it must be *responsive.* It cannot be merely acquisitive.

This attitude to knowing God takes us into the area of personal relationships at the start. God is not the static object of our enquiries but the One who takes the initiative in making himself known. When we apprehend his activity aright, we begin to seek him in the right way. We then want to see him by his own light and not just by our own. We begin to make the great discoveries which will revolutionize our thinking. We begin to see him as he really is in his goodness, purity and righteousness – and to see ourselves as we really are in our sinfulness and need of him. We are brought to a position where God can lead us on to a true and saving knowledge of himself in the Son he gave for the salvation of our world.

Our knowledge of God will be responsive: the joyful discovery that he knows us and wants us to know him; that knowing him is the greatest thing in life, in this world and the next:

---

[11] Ibid., I.ii.1.

This is what the LORD says:
'Let not the wise man boast of his wisdom
    or the strong man boast of his strength
    or the rich man boast of his riches,
but let him who boasts boast about this:
    that he understands and knows me,
that I am the LORD, who exercises kindness,
    justice and righteousness on earth,
    for in these I delight,'
declares the LORD.[12]

Apart from such joyful knowledge as this, knowing whether or not there is a God becomes a pointless exercise. Worse, it becomes the impudent affirmation of our priority over him, the priority of our curiosity about his existence over the character of the God who exists, and whose existence presses in on us on every side, challenging us at every level of our being: physical, personal, mental and moral.

3. The need for special revelation

While God has left his signature on creation, and while, to use a phrase of Jonathan Edwards, he communicates 'a sort of shadow … of his excellencies' in its beauty and intricacy, we can never by this arrive at the proper knowledge of God. There is a gulf between ourselves and God which can be bridged only from the divine side. The message of Scripture is that God *has* crossed that gulf and made himself known, not vaguely but specifically, not just

---

[12] Jer. 9:23–24.

informatively but savingly, in words of his choice to people of his choice.

Calvin likened God's use of human speech to the simplicities of baby-talk between a mother and her child – but it is baby-talk which stretches us to the utmost! Human language may not be adequate to say everything about God. It is adequate, however, for the purposes for which it was given, and it is adequate, if he chooses, to bring to us the personal self-revelation of the God who is Father, Son and Holy Spirit. If God chooses such talk, our philosophy of language and being must not despise it.

Part of our sinful arrogance is to think we can arrive at the knowledge of God without his word. But because of sin, natural theology ('human reasoning about God, under the conditions of sin, unaided by special revelation')[13] leaves us, still, with God as an unknown God.[14] We need the special revelation of the Scriptures, the revelation of himself which God gave to the patriarchs and prophets, which is confirmed by the witness of the Spirit in the hearts of God's people and which bears within itself its own authentication. Indeed, says Calvin, 'no-one can get even the slightest taste of right and sound doctrine unless he be a pupil of Scripture' without which we fall into error.[15]

> Just as old or bleary-eyed men and those with weak vision, if you thrust before them a most beautiful volume, even if they recognise it to be some sort of writing, yet can scarcely construe two words, but with the aid of spectacles will begin to

---

[13] Calvin *(Institutes)*, I.v.12, fn. 41.
[14] Acts 17:23.
[15] Calvin *(Institutes)*, I.vi.2.

read distinctly; so Scripture, gathering up the otherwise confused knowledge of God in our minds, having dispersed our
dullness, clearly shows us the true God. This, therefore, is a
special gift, where God, to instruct the church, not merely uses
mute teachers, but also opens his most hallowed lips.[16]

If we turn aside from this, in favour of our own ideas of
what God is or should be, we shall never reach the goal of
knowing God. Even Paul called the splendour of the divine countenance 'unapproachable',[17] so that the knowledge of God 'is for us like an inexplicable labyrinth unless
we are conducted into it by the thread of the Word; so that
it is better to limp along this path than to dash with all
speed outside it'.[18]

There is no rivalry here between the word of God as
Scripture and the Word made flesh as Jesus Christ. The
Word he is and the word he speaks are one Word: the
unfolding self-revelation of God, begin-fling with the creation and reaching its climax in the person and work of
Jesus Christ, his incarnation, atoning death and vindicating
resurrection and exaltation. We meet the Word in his word
– Old Testament and New. Alister McGrath pays due
attention to Calvin's emphasis on Scripture and writes:

> Christianity is Christ-centred, not book-centred; if it appears
> to be book-centred, it is because it is through the words of
> Scripture that the believer encounters and feeds upon Jesus
> Christ. Scripture is a means not an end; a channel, rather than
> what is channelled. Calvin's preoccupation with human

---

[16] Ibid., I.vi.1.
[17] 1 Tim. 6:16.
[18] Calvin *(Institutes)*, I.vi.3.

language and supremely with the text of Scripture, reflects his fundamental conviction that it is here, through reading and meditating upon this text, that it is possible to encounter and experience the risen Christ. A concentration upon the means reflects the crucial importance which Calvin attaches to the end. To suggest that Calvin – or, indeed, anyone who pays high regard to God's self-revelation in and through Scripture – is a 'bibliolater', one who worships a book, is to betray a culpable lack of insight into Calvin's concerns and methods.[19]

4. The historic Christ

The Christian faith centres on a person who, on any account, remains one of the most powerful influences in world history. The historicity of Jesus of Nazareth is undoubted, except perhaps by a minority. There are near-contemporary references in the writings of the Roman historian, Tacitus, and the Jewish historian, Josephus. We have well over 5,000 ancient manuscripts of parts or the whole of books which now comprise our New Testament which go back to the fifth, fourth, third, and second centuries AD. It is one of the phenomena of history that the ancient world is littered with evidence of Jesus of Nazareth and the communities he founded. The earliest is a part of John's Gospel which palaeographers confidently date about AD 125, that is within 90 years of the events it records –astonishingly close in historical terms. Yet when this manuscript was copied, there were already Christian churches, communities of the resurrection, in existence. That existence we can trace back further still.

---

[19] McGrath, op. cit., pp. 28–29.

5. The risen Lord

The apostle Paul wrote his first letter to the Corinthians in about AD 52 or 53, about twenty years after Jesus' death. His claim in 1 Corinthians 15:1–11 that the various disciples and followers of Jesus had encountered him after his crucifixion as the risen Lord, could easily have been falsified by those who remembered the time and by the original followers of Jesus themselves. They could have said, 'It wasn't like that.' But they were preaching the same thing!

Moreover, Paul himself had been preaching this for eighteen years before he wrote to the Corinthians. It had been the central message of his long evangelistic and missionary career from the start. That takes us back to his Damascus road encounter with the exalted Christ and his immediate preaching in the local synagogue, that Jesus is the Son of God.[20] All that was just a year or two after the event and easily falsifiable at that stage.[21] So, by stages, the surprising facticity of the Christian message can be supported. By that I mean its nature as concrete fact in history; not mysticism, not philosophy, not even therapy!

The evidences for the resurrection of Christ are well known and they form a formidable body of proof, especially when the 'explanations' are examined and found to be inadequate: the empty tomb and the inability of the

---

[20] Acts 9:20.

[21] Leon Morris writes: 'George Ogg dates the crucifixion as AD 33 and Paul's conversion as AD 34 or 35 *(The Chronology of the Life of Paul* [London, 1968], p. 200) and Martin Hengel likewise dates his conversion as AD 32–34 *(Between Jesus and Paul* [Philadelphia, 1983], p. 11), and N. A. Dahl puts it "only a couple of years after Christ's death" *(Studies in Paul* [Minneapolis, 1977], p. 2)' (Morris [1988], p. 534).

authorities to produce the body, the credible witnesses who were not expecting it but spent a lifetime preaching it, the resurrection 'appearances' themselves (not shimmering visions but concrete encounters and sustained seminars!), the impossibility of groups of people having the same hallucination, the improbability of a not-quite-dead and severely wounded Jesus convincing his disciples that he was Lord over death (not to mention walking the seven miles to Emmaus on recently crucified ankles and appearing behind locked doors). In such a scenario, if Jesus had not died, his integrity would have done.

6. The claims of Jesus

And that brings us to the most stubborn fact of all: a Jesus who says, 'I am meek and lowly of heart', and who yet says, 'Before Abraham was, I am.'[22] Jesus is a prophet who does not point away to God, but who preaches a gospel of 'I ams'; who claims to be the centre of history and the Judge at its end, 'that all may honour the Son just as they honour the Father';[23] and who sends his disciples out to 'make disciples of all nations, baptising them in the name of the Father and of the Son and of the Holy Spirit'.[24] Who is this who shares the honours with God, who speaks of a life and a glory with his Father 'before the world began', and who accepts the worship of the disciples and the confession of Thomas, 'My Lord and my God'?[25]

---

[22] John 8:58.

[23] John 5:23.

[24] Matt. 28:19.

[25] John 17:5; 20:28.

Here in space-time history is a fellow human being, of
undoubted godliness and integrity, who says 'All things
have been committed to me by my Father. No-one knows
the Son except the Father, and no-one knows the Father
except the Son and those to whom the Son chooses to
reveal him.'[26]

It is not convincing to say that all this was put into the
mouth of a harmless young rabbi by over-zealous disciples.
To say that the Jesus of the New Testament is largely the
creation of his admirers is to say that he was ordinary and
they were extra-ordinary, he was pedestrian and they were
sublime, he was parochial and they were magnificent. It is
to have a boring Jesus and an exciting church (my experience has been otherwise!). It is to have the Sermon on the
Mount, the parables of the kingdom, and the drama of
Calvary and the resurrection created by fishermen turned
lay-preachers and first-century schools of thought. Shake-
speare by committee is nothing to it! But in fact it is Jesus
who towers over them all, who has not been dwarfed by
2,000 years of on-going human history, who has changed
the lives of millions, and who has sown the Western world
with many of its (better) values.

The fact is that the Jesus the New Testament writers
portray is not at all the kind of Jesus they would have
invented. He was a different kind of messiah, preaching a
different kind of kingdom to a different kind of people
than anyone expected. It was he who shaped them, not
they who shaped him. They wrote and lived in the impact
of his uniqueness. What they would have invented would
have been, at best, devoutly commonplace. Their fictional
Jesus would never have spoken words which often seemed

---

[26] Matt. 11:27.

quite blasphemous to his critics. He would have been the model penitent not the sinless Son, the modest preacher of a message bigger than himself or the hero of messianic expectations who was tragically lost to Israel and the world.

But in fact he puzzled them, shocked them and far surpassed them with his claims. And when he died they did not understand or expect, or even, at first, believe in his resurrection from the dead. And when they did, they worshipped and served him with joy and great assurance all their lives.

That assurance we too can have – about God, about forgiveness, and about eternal life – if we listen to him and believe in him. No-one meets the deepest needs of our flawed and dying humanity like the Christ who said, 'Come to me, all you who are weary and burdened, and I will give you rest … the Son of Man did not come to be served, but to serve, and to give his life as a ransom for many … I am the good shepherd. The good shepherd lays down his life for the sheep … My sheep listen to my voice; I know them, and they follow me. I give them eternal life, and they shall never perish; no-one can snatch them out of my hand … Do not be afraid. I am the First and the Last. I am the Living One; I was dead, and behold I am alive for ever and ever! And I hold the keys of death and Hades.'[27]

There have always been godly men and women who seem in particular ways to reflect God's character strongly and clearly. But Jesus is not simply one in that category of persons nor did his apostles present him as such. The New Testament does not say 'Jesus is like God', it says 'God is like Jesus'; it says that to see Jesus is to see God, to come to

---

[27] Matt. 11:28; Mark 10:45; John 10:11, 27–28; Rev. 1:17–18.

Jesus is to come to God, to be judged by Jesus will be to be judged by God. In a word, there will be nothing in God, no attribute or quality, no decision or purpose, that is not in Jesus Christ, the Son of God, the one in whom 'all the fulness of the Deity lives in bodily form'.[28] If we know and are right with the Son, we need not fear to stand before the Father. There will be no hidden menace, no terrible discovery, no final contradiction of our hopes, for, as A. M. Ramsay once put it, recalling 1 John 1:5, 'God is Christ like and in him is no unChristlikeness at all.'[29]

7. The inspired Scriptures

Yet, notwithstanding all this, Jesus did not come as the first and only witness to the Living God but pointed to a long unfolding revelation by God to Abraham, Moses and the prophets. He himself fulfilled much of that and in his own person and teaching took it to new heights. He never relegated, however, what we call the 'Old Testament' Scriptures to a lower level of inspiration or authority than his own words. On the contrary, he taught its divine authorship and abiding validity.[30] So did his apostles, the first and foremost teachers of the church, themselves writing inspired Scriptures for that ongoing church.[31]

The apostle Paul, having congratulated Timothy on his early education in the Old Testament, says 'All Scripture is

---

[28] Col. 2:9.

[29] Cited in John V. Taylor, *The Christ-like God* (SCM, 1992), fly-leaf.

[30] Matt. 5:17–18; 22:41–45; Luke 22:25–28, 44; cf. John 14:26; 16:12–14.

[31] 2 Tim.3:14–17; 2 Pet.1:19–21; 3:1–2, 15–16.

God-breathed and is useful for teaching, rebuking, cor-
recting and training in righteousness.'[32] Peter also
expressly states that the prophets delivered a message that
they were given, not a philosophy, or even a theology,
that they had invented: 'Above all, you must understand
that no prophecy of Scripture came about by the prophet's
own interpretation. For prophecy never had its origin in
the will of man, but men spoke from God as they were
carried along by the Holy Spirit.'[33] The prophets themselves continually made just this point and we read phrases
like 'The word of the Lord came', 'Thus says the Lord' and
'The burden of the Lord' no fewer than 3,808 times!

It is this *objectivity* in the Christian faith, the objective
revelation of God in Jesus Christ and also in the entire
unfolding revelation of God in the Scriptures, both Old
and New Testaments, that counters the extreme subjectiv-
ism of our age, whether we encounter it in existentialism,
New Age mysticism, or the gentle but fatal cynicism of
Woody Allen. However, that does not shut us up to a mere
scholasticism, or to a purely intellectual recognition of the
Scriptures. There has to be a work of God in us as well as
beyond us if we are to know God, the God of the Scriptures, the God of the prophets and the apostles, the God
and Father of our Lord Jesus Christ.

8. The need of God's Spirit

Corresponding to his work in the writers of scripture is
the work of the Holy Spirit bearing testimony in the

---

[32] 2 Tim. 3:16.
[33] Pet. 1:20–21.

hearts of all God's people, sophisticated and simple, that
this is the word of the Lord. The Scriptures do not de-
rive their authority from the church, notwithstanding
its work in recognizing the canon, but the church itself
is 'built on the foundation of the apostles and prophets'.[34] Scripture exhibits evidence of its own truth and
'the highest proof of Scripture derives in general from
the fact that God in person speaks in it.

This was an important point in Calvin's theology of the
Word:

> If we desire to provide in the best way for our consciences –
> that they may not be perpetually beset by the instability of
> doubt or vacillation, and that they may not also boggle at the
> smallest quibbles – we ought to seek our conviction in a higher
> place than human reasons, judgements or conjectures, that is,
> in the secret testimony of the Spirit ... The testimony of the
> Spirit is more excellent than all reason. For as God alone is a fit
> witness of himself in his Word, so also the Word will not find
> acceptance in men's hearts before it is sealed by the inward tes-
> timony of the Spirit. The same Spirit, therefore, who has spo-
> ken through the mouths of the prophets must penetrate into
> our hearts to persuade us that they faithfully proclaimed what
> had been divinely commanded.[35]

Scripture, says Calvin, as the Word of God, is 'self-authen-
ticated' but 'the certainty it deserves with us, it attains by
the testimony of the Spirit':

> For even if it wins reverence for itself by its own majesty, it se-
> riously affects us only when it is sealed to our hearts through

---

[34] Eph. 2:20.
[35] Calvin *(Institutes)*, I.vii.4.

the Spirit. Therefore, illumined by his power, we believe neither by our own nor by anyone else's judgement that Scripture
is from God; but above human judgement we affirm with utter certainty (just as if we were gazing upon the majesty of God
himself) that it has flowed to us from the very mouth of God
by the ministry of men... Let us, then, know that the only true
faith is that which the Spirit of God seals on our hearts . . .
Whenever, then, the fewness of believers disturbs us, let the
converse come to mind, that only those to whom it is given
can comprehend the mysteries of God (cf. Matt. 13:11).[36]

9. The people who listen

God is a speaking God – and a speaking God calls for a
listening people. This book seeks to listen to God's voice
in Scripture, to explore and apply the revelation of himself that God has made in Scripture to ourselves and our
times. The listening posture is crucial for all knowledge
of God from first to last; it is the natural posture of faith.
Anselm of Canterbury described theological enquiry as
'Faith seeking understanding'. Anselm believed that
faith was a necessary foundation and support for all further discovery. He wrote, in famous words: 'I do not seek
to understand that I may believe, but I believe that I may
understand: this I also believe, that unless I believe I will
not understand.'[37]

This belief is not an eyes-shut leap in the dark, but a profound Spirit-wrought recognition of and response to the
call of God which brings us to our knees in gratitude and

---

[36] Ibid., I.vii.5.
[37] Anselm, *Proslogion,* i.

adoration.[38] Jesus put it most simply and memorably: 'My sheep listen to my voice; I know them, and they follow me.'[39] Helmut Thielicke wrote, 'What we call our knowledge of Christ is imparted to us only as we achieve a relationship of trust in him.'[40] The human desire to understand God in a non-relational way is a profound expression of our fallenness. 'The first task of theology is to bring us to his feet.'[41] It is with such a conviction that this book is written, with the prayer that it may be used to keep us at the feet of God.

---

[38] Matt. 11:25; 16:17; 1 Cor. 2:8–16.

[39] John 10:27.

[40] Quoted in Donald McCullough, *The Trivialisation of God: The dangerous illusion of a manageable deity* (NavPress, 1995), p. 71.

[41] Thomas Howard and J. I. Packer, *Christianity: The true humanism* (Word, 1985), p. 68.

No Compromise

Melody Green

Dynamic and charismatic, singer/songwriter Keith Green challenged believers to break out of their status quo Christianity and embrace a 'put-it-all-on-the-line' life of faith and action.

When Keith was just 28, a tragic aeroplane crash took him and two of his young children home to the Lord. Yet his music and ministry still affects many today.

In this inspiring biography, Keith's wife Melody shares their years of spiritual searching, the events that led them to Jesus, and how their dedication to minister to others began.

A gifted songwriter herself, many will have sung Melody's 'There is a Redeemer'. She is also a well-known speaker and author.

Harvest House Publishers
ISBN: 0-73690-319-4

Price: £5.99

£4.99 with money off voucher

Chapter 1

"One Day You're Up..."

Anything can happen on the streets of Hollywood I'd seen some pretty wild things, but never anything so bizarre as what I saw one night on Ventura Boulevard

As Keith and I walked out of The Bla Bla Cafe, a blast of hot night air hit us in the face. It was after 2:00 A.M., but the Street was still awake with activity. Four drag queens swept by us, followed by a couple in disco outfits, all headed inside for a late-night breakfast. Next door the watchdogs at Bruno's Corvette Repairs were pacing inside their chain-linked fence, barking at everything that moved — including us. Keith had played three sets tonight, and we were headed for home, exhausted. I was glad to see "Victor von Van," our VW with its hippie-style, Indian print curtains, parked at the curb.

Keith had been performing at The Bla — as it was affectionately known to its regulars — for almost a year. It was a small showcase nightclub in the San Fernando Valley, just down the road from Hollywood. The Bla spotlighted showbiz hopefuls and was frequented by talent scouts from big record companies. Keith was one of those hopefuls. But tonight he'd given it his all one more time—and now we were leaving, still undiscovered.

As Keith walked around the front of the van, I opened the passenger door. That was when we spotted a figure looming toward us out of the dark. It was Harmony.

Harmony looked like a gruff mountain man with his brown, scraggly hair and beard. Here we were in 1974, but this guy struck us as someone caught in a '60s time warp. He was calm and easy. All he talked about was peace, love, and living off the land. He wasn't a close friend, but he and Keith had gotten stoned together once.

"Hey, how's it goin'?" Keith called. He shut his door again and stepped back on the sidewalk.

Sleepily I leaned my head back, knowing I was in for a wait. Inevitably most of our conversations drifted toward spiritual experiences these days. Keith and I had tried a lot of things — a lot of things. Recently we'd been curious about Jesus. We weren't Christians. Church was a dead institution to us. But Jesus did seem to be a spiritual Master of some sort, and we had a degree of respect for his life and teachings.

Sure enough, Keith and Harmony immediately began talking about the supernatural. It was just a typical conversation — for people who were into drugs and the mystical, which were a lot of the people we knew.

"I've been reading about Jesus lately," Keith was saying. "He was a pretty radical person."

Harmony's eyes seemed to brighten. Then, slowly, a strange look came over his face. His eyes got misty and distant. Very calmly he said, "I am Jesus Christ."

Keith reacted like he'd been stung by a scorpion. Without missing a beat he shot back, "Beware of the false prophets who come to you in sheep's clothing, but inwardly are ravenous wolves!" I recognized the quote as something Jesus had said. What happened next was really hard to believe.

Harmony's eyes grew wide. Then they narrowed to slits. Furrows creased across his forehead, and his bushy eyebrows knit together. A sneer came over his usually mild face, and his upper lip curled back, exposing yellow, smoke-stained teeth. Leaning toward Keith, his teeth bared, he let out a growl that started in the throat, like that of a wolf, and ended with the horrible hissing sound of a snake.

It happened in only seconds. Harmony's face relaxed. But his eyes looked confused. Embarrassed. The hiss seemed to hang in the still night air.

My skin was still tingling from the shock. Keith had obviously been rocked by it too. He looked from Harmony to me with wide eyes. This was Hollywood, but things like this only happened in the movies. I wondered what Keith was thinking.

It was like someone or something took control of Harmony momentarily, using him for its own purposes. Then just as quickly it discarded him, leaving him to pick up the pieces in confused embarrassment. Dazed, Harmony mumbled something. But Keith quickly excused himself, jumped into Victor, and shoved the key in the ignition.

As we drove home over the dark streets we kept looking at each other in disbelief. Keith was more animated than usual. He kept saying, "Did he really do that? I can't believe it!"

We talked about nothing else until we crawled into bed and fell asleep, sometime after 3:30 A.M.

The weird experience with Harmony did have one major effect on us. It brought some things into sharp focus. Namely, that there was, indeed, a very real spiritual realm — a realm full of power and possibly even danger. We were just coming to a deeper realization that there must be spiritual forces beyond our knowing. Had we heard a voice from that other side, speaking through Harmony? Or was it just the voice of the age? After all, a lot of musicians, artists, and writers – the "beautiful" people – were saying things like, "You are your own god. There is no right or wrong."

But we wondered: Is there a dark side and a light side to spiritual energy?

Keith and I had both been caught up in a search to find our spiritual identities for some time. We were looking for truth – whatever it was – and our search for light had taken us both on many strange paths, from Buddhism to stuff like astral projection and, of course, drugs. We were both convinced the truth was hidden out there somewhere like a pearl in the ocean, and when we found it, it would fill an empty spot in our hearts. It would make life really worth living. Until then every day held the potential of being the day of the great revelation.

At the time of our weird encounter with Harmony, however, we'd been slipping a bit, losing hope, even dabbling with the drugs again that we'd sworn off but kept falling back into. Our spiritual ambitions never kept us out of the fog for long. In fact, the constant lure of those other voices had pretty well convinced us there was a dark and a light side. After Harmony's eruption, Keith, with his usual all-or-nothing manner, was determined to know how to tell the difference. Although we never forgot the incident outside

The Bla, there were more pressing matters. Like Keith's all-consuming dream.

In particular, our whole life revolved around Keith's drive to make it big in the music business. Now that he was performing at The Bla, we lived with the constant hunger that the right person would walk in one night and discover Keith Green.

The Bla was just down Ventura Boulevard from The Queen Mary, and Keith's audience was always seasoned with gays and straights alike. Neither camp seemed to mind the other. To be honest, it was often difficult to tell who belonged where. The biggest standouts were the drag queens, sweeping in wearing satin dresses, jangly jewels, and high-styled wigs. Only their exaggerated feminine gestures and five o'clock shadows shining through heavy layers of make up betrayed their true gender.

Keith's family and my mom lived here in Southern California. But The Bla was like a second home to us. The people like family. Even though Keith's last set ended at 1:00A.M., we often stayed until Albie, the owner, closed the doors three hours later. Keith and Albie would lift a table onto the empty stage and we'd get a foursome together, shuffling the cards for a lot of laughs and a hot game of Bid-Whist. Sometimes a gang from The Bla got together on Sunday afternoons to play softball.

Albie, who was in his forties, took pride in running a successful club and rubbing shoulders with the almost-elite of Hollywood's underside. He doted like a mother hen over his performers and expected the audience to give each act full attention. Albie also had become a friend and mentor to Keith. That's why his sudden ultimatum threw Keith for such a loop.

It came one Wednesday night after Keith's third set. People wise, the turnout had been disappointing. Wednesday wasn't the greatest night, of course, but it was a start. Albie's eyes were kind, and his manner fatherly as usual, when he came up to our table. Then he lowered the boom.

"I'm sorry, Keith, but you've got two weeks to pack 'em in or I'll have to replace you with another act."

"You're kidding," Keith said in surprise. I felt a stab of rejection too.

"I'm not," Albie said. "If you want your own night you gotta draw more people. I've got a club to run. Salaries to pay. I'm sorry, Keith, but I just can't afford to keep losing money on you."

We couldn't believe our ears. Keith went home that night deeply depressed. Even the Quaalude he took to soothe his bruised feelings couldn't touch the real hurt — the whispers of failure. It seemed to me that the worst part about performing was having to sell yourself. Being so vulnerable. When you don't mea sure up, nothing eases the sickening feeling that maybe it's not just your act that isn't good enough. Maybe it's you.

After Albie's ultimatum Keith sprang into immediate action. He was never one to take a challenge lying down. Starting on Thursday, he spent all week phoning everyone and anyone he knew. He almost begged them to come, telling them about all his new songs, how he wanted to see them, and how he was going to lose his job unless the place was packed. I felt embarrassed for him, and even worse when he insisted I call my friends as well! But we were in a terrible bind.

Keith had already pitched himself to every major record label in town. That resulted in some nibbles. One company had flown us to New York. Nothing materialized. Keith even tried to sing on a Grand Funk soundalike record, but didn't sound enough alike. There were some more nibbles but not bites.

Money was tight and getting tighter. We'd already sold

my red Triumph sports car and my prized Martin D-35 guitar. My savings account had breathed its last. So to supplement our small income from The Bla – sometimes less than $15 – Keith clenched his teeth and played proms, parties, and banquets. It was the bottom of the barrel for any serious artist, but the word for us in 1974 was survival. And now the threat of getting fired from The Bla Bla – a small-potatoes club as Hollywood nightspots go – would be the final humiliation.

The following Wednesday, we walked into The Bla about 8:30 P.M., feeling quiet apprehension. I looked around and was struck with how empty this place could look.

The Bla was dark and narrow inside, with a small stage to the right as you walked in the front door. The bar, which was too small for anyone to sit at, ran across the back, right in front of the tiny, one-man kitchen. The most consistent thing about the decor was its inconsistency. Absolutely nothing matched. Between the stage and the bar was a collection of banged-up wooden tables. On the walls huge dragonflies in vivid yellows and oranges hung beside oversized photos autographed by "sorta knowns."

When packed The Bla could hold about 85 people on chrome-and-vinyl chairs, the kind you'd find around a Formica table in someone's kitchen in the 1950s. Right now those chairs were mostly empty.

Only a few patrons sat in quiet conversation as Keith nervously eyed the stage. Albie was getting a check ready at one of the tables. The cook and the two waiters, Eddie and Mr. Sally, were at the back bar, the only others in the whole place. Albie caught Keith's eye. Neither one said anything, but it was a knowing glance. Tonight was it.

Keith and I sat silently in the back of the skinny little

club, watching each other watch the door. We certainly looked like West Coast musicians, if nothing else. Married for only eight months, we made quite a pair. Me in an Indian print skirt, embroidered gauze blouse, and long straight hair. And Keith, wearing blue jeans and a new flowered cowboy shirt. His long, curly ponytail had recently been left on the hair stylist's floor. What remained had been layered into a new California style called The Shag—short for shaggy. Even freshly cut, his hair still hung well below his shoulders. I silently admired his new professional image. Less hippie, but still very hip.

Slowly, in twos and threes, people started arriving. One cigarette after another was lit, and spirals of blue smoke curled gracefully to the ceiling. As the chairs filled, the noise level began to rise. Chairs scraped against the cement floor. Loud laughter punctuated conversations. Eddie, the head waiter, clipped his orders to the revolving wheel, and the smell and sizzle of burgers drifted from the tiny kitchen.

Still there weren't enough people and we knew it. Mr. Sally stepped over to our table to take my order, wearing his usual uniform – a custom-made T shirt with a sketch of him in a bouffant hairdo and "Mr. Sally" scrawled across the front in fancy white script. In the low light, the black cotton stretching tightly across his ebony skin threatened to cast him into obscurity except for a few well-placed rhinestones. I wasn't very hungry so I ordered Guac-and-Papa's – fried potato slices with a bowl of guacamole. *Would any of our friends bother to show up?* Keith's first hour-long set started at 9:00 P.M. We had only ten minutes to go. Keith's right leg was bouncing nervously. He was all raw energy and ready to start. More tense minutes ticked by.

"Do I look OK?" he asked, poking at his hair.

"You look great, honey," I assured him.

I loved the way Keith looked. His clear blue eyes and fair skin gave him a pure, almost childlike air. Now that he'd shaved off his beard, the fact that he was just 20 years old was much more evident.

"It's 8:58," Keith said, breaking into my thoughts. "Where is everybody?" He was all wound up and ready to pop.

I tried to calm him down a bit. "They'll be here in a few minutes," I responded, trying to conceal my own fears. "We've got a little more time."

"There is no more time. This is it." Keith shoved back his chair with disappointment written all over him. Yet I sensed his determination. He was a fighter, and even though the odds were against him I knew Keith would give it his all.

Albie had started to pace in the back as Keith made his way to the stage and sat at the battered upright piano. He squinted into the single spotlight and, leaning toward the microphone, spoke in mock military fashion.

"I'd like the sergeant of arms to call the room to attention! Ladies and gentlemen, and *others*, I'd like to interrupt your rambling conversation for some music."

Keith started noodling on the piano, but few people in the scant crowd paid attention. Keith fidgeted in his seat while his fingers wandered over the keys for a few moments. I could tell he was trying to figure out what to play. He finally launched into "Life Goes On," a song he'd just written with his new friend Randy Stonehill:

> *Marvin was a connoisseur of twenty-cent wine.*
> *You could see him bummin' nickels down on Sunset*
>   *and Vine.*

One day his wealthy uncle passed away in Bel Air
And now he's sippin' from a vintage year
Marvin's sip pin from a vintage year.

Then the chorus:

Life goes on and the world goes 'round.
One day you're up, the next day you're down.
Don't count on good luck, there's nothing to say except,
"Thank you, Lord, for another day!"

The funny lyrics and funky rhythm grabbed everyone's attention. Keith pounded the keys in a way that sent terror into the heart of every piano teacher he ever had. I often held my breath hoping he wouldn't miss a note, but even when he did it didn't matter. It wasn't perfection that drew you to Keith's music, or to him for that matter. It was heart.

A few more tables were filling up, and to my relief some people were clapping along. Keith paused to do what came naturally — give more directions: "Here's the second verse. But you don't really have to pay attention to the verses. They're just there to keep the choruses coming. OK, here we go!"

There was a famous senator that everyone knew.
One day a sly reporter found a girl in his room.
The reelection survey said that he'd make a kill
But now he's washing dishes down at Joe's Bar and Grill.
He makes his famous speeches now at Joe's Bar and Grill!

The chorus came around again and people began to sing with enthusiasm, imitating Keith's comical gestures. Keith sang, "One day you're up," pointing to the ceiling. Then he plunged his thumb toward the floor as he shook his head and sang, "Next day you're down...." The night was coming alive.

Eddie danced his orders down the narrow aisles, balancing trays of shish kebabs, burgers, and beer above his head. Mr. Sally ran a fork across the soda fountain grates with the zest of a marimba player, and I kept rhythm by playing my water glass with a spoon. Captured by Keith's enthusiasm, hoots, hollers, and hand claps erupted around the room — and more tables filled while he played his next few songs.

I had yet to see any of our friends. Then a movement at the door caught my eye. It was our friend Michelle Brandes, the youth and family leader at a local Jewish synagogue. I recognized her even in the dim light. A birth defect had left her with a pronounced limp. She made her way slowly through the smoky haze and sat beside me.

Still, I was paying far more attention to the door than to Keith. Then he kicked into a Joni Mitchell song, "Free Man in Paris," and I could tell he was starting to relax a little. Since I was wondering where all our friends were I felt especially tuned-in to the message of the song.

"Free Man in Paris" tells the story of a record company executive on vacation in Paris, tired of cranking out hit artists — "stoking the starmaker machinery behind the popular song." Another part of the lyrics says: "I was a free man in Paris, I felt unfettered and alive. Nobody calling me up for favors, nobody's future to decide."

Keith had become all too familiar with the starmaker machinery: the record companies, producers, publishers, and agents — all fighting over "who gets what" of various royalty rights. When an artist becomes a hit, he's a hot property and then every body "loves him" as they clamor

for a piece of the pie. Until then, though, you just look for
connections and wait for your big break. The gears of the
machinery are oiled with the tears of countless hopeful
artists who never get their break. I loved Joni Mitchell's
music, and this song was one of my favorites. But it also
made me shudder

Keith's fear of not succeeding was overshadowed only
by the fear of blowing it – of getting involved with the
wrong people out of desperation.

As I glanced around the smoky room I thought,
*Someone could be here right now who could help Keith in a big
way.* But then there were some people whose help we defi-
nitely didn't want.

Like the guy last September. He heard Keith at The Bla
and just flipped. Keith later met with him in his fancy Hollywood office, and the guy bubbled over with
"I-can-make-you-a-star" noises. Here was a voice promis-
ing the success and stardom Keith wanted. But, as Keith
confided in his daily journal, a log he kept for years, there
was – as usual – a string attached:

> *He's very rich and he has a big name in the business.*
> *He's also incredibly gay and I felt him vibing on me.*
> *Even though he could do a lot for me – bread and contact*
> *wise – I gave a "nay" to working with him.*

And that wasn't the first time a record company executive
tried to hit on Keith. Then there had been the movie score
with a popular director, but a pretty sleazy movie even by
our standards. The more Keith got into it, the more he
wanted out. Things soured on the money end, too. Keith
had finished the music for two reels when he quit the pro-
ject. In his journal he said it fell through "due to cheapness

and underhanded tactics on their part, and lack of true desire on mine." That was another problem – Keith's high standards.

As Michelle and I watched Keith now, I couldn't help but think that maybe he would have been discovered already if he'd just been a bit more flexible. But for Keith some things were set in concrete. His dad had been his manager for years and had instilled very high standards in him. If something didn't feel right, Keith wasn't going to do it, and that was that. His high principles were admirable, but secretly I was afraid he might he just a little too picky for his own good.

As Keith continued on with the next few songs, he squinted through the glaring stage light, keeping a check on the crowd. A few more people filtered in. Several faithful friends made a two hour drive from the desert in Lancaster, Keith's parents came to cheer him on – and another friend, Karen Bender, had even brought her daughter Dawn, who had the longest braids I'd ever seen on a little kid. I was disappointed that Todd Fishkind, Keith's best friend, wasn't able to come, but our poker-playing buddies from Marina del Rey showed and so did a few industry friends.

Keith played for another 20 minutes before taking his first break. He finished to an enthusiastic round of applause and joy fully jumped off the stage, his blue eyes sparkling with the victory of the moment.

A full house!

As he walked over to the table, sweat glistening on his face, excitement made his usually springy steps even springier. Not only were we high on the moment, but our friend Harriet had come bearing gifts.

Harriet shoved a shoe box toward Keith.

"Shoes?"

"Open it," she said with a sly smile.

Keith lifted the lid. His eyes brightened. "Brownies!"

"My own special recipe," Harriet said, winking. "Homegrown, if you know what I mean."

"You put grass in them?"

"The best."

"Eddie! Hey, Eddie! Bring me a large milk."

Keith grabbed a handful of the marijuana-laced goodies and passed the box to some select friends in a ritual of sharing the wealth, patterned after Indians passing the peace pipe. We made the rounds, telling everyone we were glad they came.

As the brownies hit bottom things began to look even more up. The strain left Keith's eyes, and he was obviously soaring with the moment.

Aihie walked up, smiling broadly. He slapped Keith on the back and said: "You did it, kid. A great night! I'm happy for you."

Keith's face was one big grin. "Yeah? So when do I get Saturdays?"

Albie chuckled and shook his head. The question didn't demand an answer, not immediately. But Keith already had his eyes on the future, on something far beyond a big night of his own at The Bla Bla Cafe.

When Keith started his second set, the haze, clinking glasses, and melodic piano all merged as my mind started to drift. I stared at the funny dragonflies on the wall—savoring the feeling of success

Somehow, though, my thoughts were pulled to our future and what might lie ahead. I just knew Keith was supposed to be up in front of a lot of people – people who were being moved by his music and what he had to say. But the problem was it wasn't clear even to Keith exactly what he had to say. He just felt he had a message to share with the world, something from his spiritual search. An important message. But what?

By the time Keith finished his third set that evening a decided victory was won. It was one of Keith's best nights yet. Driving home I was still hyped from the excitement of the evening – and Harriet's tasty brownies. My mind was hung up on a million questions: Was this the beginning of a big break for Keith? Was he finally on a roll? Why did someone like Keith, who was loaded with talent, need to resort to begging his friends to come hear him play? It seemed like such a contradiction, hut then again there were lots of contradictions in our lives.

In areas like honesty and integrity it seemed Keith had the highest standards of anyone I'd ever met. We didn't cheat on our taxes, but sometimes we'd take illegal drugs. Was there a difference?

Even if Keith made it in music, would we make it as a couple? As much as we liked to talk about living in harmony with the universe and each other, we sure had our share of arguments. Big arguments.

It was hard to live with so many unanswered questions, and not just regarding Keith's career. Some of the other battles we were fighting were on an entirely different front – one that was even more vague and elusive. It was as if something was tugging at us, pulling us into uncharted waters – something that would change us forever.

In fact we had no idea we were on the verge of a break-through much bigger than we ever imagined.

All I knew at the moment was that this man I married sure had a lot of complex facets to his personality. In the days following our victory at The Bla, my mind wandered over the many strands that wove together inside him. I thought about the sensitive inner man who was determined to find spiritual answers. Yet there was another side of him — the little boy who always wanted to be in show business. The little boy side explained so much about who Keith was now. But did it offer any clues about where we were going?

The Last Days according to Jesus

R. C. Sproul

What did Jesus teach on Mount Olivet? Who is the Antichrist? What did John teach in Revelation?

In the 'Last Days according to Jesus', respected theologian R. C. Sproul focuses on what Jesus himself taught about the last days and the timing of his return.

Sproul answers critics who claim Christ's teaching was 'defective' and addresses several key questions regarding the last days.

As one reviewer wrote:

'You owe it to the church and to yourself to spend time interacting with Sproul on these critical questions.'

Dr Sproul is professor of systematic theology and apologetics at Knox Theological Seminary and founder and chairman of Ligonier Ministries.

Baker Book House
ISBN: 0-80106-340-X

Price: £9.99

£7.99 with money off voucher

This is the spirit of Antichrist,
which you have heard was coming,
and is now already in the world.

(1 John 4:3)

Chapter 8

Who Is the Antichrist?

Perhaps there is no greater mystery associated with the New Testament record than the identity of the antichrist. The very mention of the word conjures up diabolical creatures such as "Rosemary's Baby," or of a human being of such unrestrained wickedness that the very mention of his name evokes terror. Futurists in eschatology regularly announce the latest candidate for the position of the antichrist. Jeane Dixon predicted that we will see the antichrist in our generation because he has already been born.

The term *antichrist* is introduced in the New Testament by the Apostle John. He speaks of the antichrist in his first epistle: "Little children, it is the last hour; and as you have heard that the Antichrist is coming, even now many antichrists have come, by which we know that it is the last hour. They went out from us, but they were not of us; for if they had been of us, they would have continued with us; but they went out that they might be made manifest, that none of them were of us. But you have an anointing from the Holy One, and you know all things." (1 John 2:18 – 20)

This passage includes several enigmatic elements. The first is the time-frame reference: "it is the last hour." This unique phrase is somewhat difficult to understand. We must ask the question, "This is the last hour of what?" Jesus spoke of his "hour" (Matt. 26:45), which has been interpreted to mean the hour of his death or the hour of his return to heavenly glory, both of which occurred in the first century. But here John is speaking, not of the last hour of Christ, but of the last hour of something else. Is it the last hour of the Jewish Age? Is it the last hour of world history? In other words, is it *a* last hour that has already elapsed, or is it *the* last hour of all human history?

Those who understand it to be the last hour of human history fall into two basic groups. First are biblical critics who cite this as one more example of "consistent eschatology," an eschatological expectation that failed to materialize within the predicted time-frame. Second are those who argue that "the last hour" began in New Testament times and continues to this day.

Alexander Ross says of this phrase:

It is important to remember that, according to the New Testament, with the coming of Christ, with His Death and Resurrection and Ascension, the last period of the world's history has begun. God has spoken His final message in His Son (Heb. 1:2). No event in the world's history can ever equal in epoch-making importance the coming of Christ till He comes again. The Christian era, as it has been put, is "the last on the Divine program; the next will be the coming of the Lord." That period has lasted more than 1900 years since John wrote the words before us and it may last some time yet, but, apart from its duration, it can be thought of being, in a very real sense, the last hour. It is "the last time," as [John] Calvin says, "in which all things are so completed that nothing remains except the final revelation of Christ.[1]

To understand this approach, we must distinguish between the term *last* in this interpretation and the term *final*. Perhaps a better word to express the view of Calvin cited by Ross is that it is the "main" or "chief" redemptive-historical hour, but certainly not the "final" hour.

Whatever John means by "the last hour," he regards it as present. Twice he says it *is* the last hour. He asserts that this is certain due to the presence of the antichrist. He speaks of the antichrist in both past and future tenses. On the one hand, the antichrist *is coming*. In this case that which is coming has not yet arrived. Here John speaks of the antichrist in the singular. But then he adds, "many antichrists have come." Here antichrist is plural and already present or past. Based on the past appearances of many antichrists, John says we know that it is the last hour.

The Spirit of the Antichrist

John further qualifies his teaching regarding the antichrist:

Beloved, do not believe every spirit, but test the spirits, whether they are of God; because many false prophets have

gone out into the world. By this you know the Spirit of God:
Every spirit that confesses that Jesus Christ has come in the
flesh is of God, and every spirit that does not confess that Jesus
Christ has come in the flesh is not of God. And this is the spirit
of the Antichrist, which you have heard was coming, and is
now already in the world. You are of God, little children, and
have overcome them, because He who is in you is greater than
he who is in the world.

(1 John 4:1—4)

In this text John speaks of the *spirit* of the antichrist. His
readers had heard that the antichrist *was coming,* but John
says he is in the world *now* and *already.* A crucial question,
however, is this: What is "already in the world"? Is it the
spirit of the antichrist, or the antichrist himself?

To answer this question we must consider various
factors. In the first place the Greek text does not include
the full phrase "And this is the spirit of the Antichrist." The
Greek text simply says, 'And this is of the Antichrist." In the
context John has been speaking of spirits that confess
Christ's coming in the flesh and of spirits that deny it. John
then concludes that "this is of the Antichrist." Translators
add the words *the spirit* in italics to signal to the reader that
they have added or supplied the words. Given the contex-
tual discussion concerning spirits, both positive and negative, the addition of "the spirit" seems to me to be
warranted.

More crucial is this question: What is the antecedent of
which in the phrase "which you have heard was coming,
and is now already in the world." Is John saying that, while
the antichrist's spirit is already in the world, the antichrist
himself is not yet in the world? If so, then the door is left
open for a future appearance of the antichrist at the end of

world history. This seems to be the view of the majority of
evangelical scholars.

Another possibility is that the antichrist himself, and
not merely his spirit, is already in the world during the first
century. In this case, two more options surface. One is that
the antichrist, though appearing in the world in the first
century, has continued his activity throughout world
history down to our day. This view would disqualify any
human from being the antichrist unless God accorded this
person miraculous longevity.

The other option is that *the* antichrist was present in the
world when John wrote this epistle and the antichrist's
work was limited to the first century.

Grammatically speaking, the antecedent of *which* should
be "the Antichrist," not merely "the spirit of the
Antichrist." If this is correct, then we must conclude that
the antichrist of whom John wrote appeared in the first
century.

Even if John's antichrist was a specific person in the first
century, this does not preclude the possibility of other
antichrists appearing at various times, or even continu-
ously, throughout church history. This speculation gains
at least some credence from John's reference to the
"many antichrists" (1 John 2:18) who had preceded *the*
antichrist.

Because John refers to "many antichrists," many scholars have concluded that the term *antichrist* refers not to a
specific individual or a series of individuals, but to institutions or a system of teaching linked to false prophets. Some
conclude that antichrist is a specific person by identifying
him with "the man of lawlessness" mentioned by the
Apostle Paul, or with the beast of the Book of Revelation.
But neither Paul nor the Apocalypse specifically uses the

term *antichrist*. Again, the only explicit references to the
antichrist occur in the epistles of John.

David Chilton argues that the term *antichrist* refers both
to a system of unbelief (the heresy that denied the reality of
the incarnation, particularly in the manner of early
Gnosticism), and to apostate individuals (like the
first-century heresiarch Cerinthus). "Putting all this
together," Chilton writes, "we can see that *antichrist* is a
description of both *the system of apostasy* and *individual apos-
tates.* In other words, antichrist was the fulfillment of Jesus'
prophecy that a time of great apostasy would come, when
'many will fall away and will betray one another and hate
one another. And many false prophets will arise, and will
mislead many' (Matt. 24:10—11).... When the doctrine of
antichrist is understood, it fits in perfectly with what the
rest of the New Testament tells us about the age of the 'ter-
minal generation.'"[2]

G.C. Berkouwer summarizes the debate by saying: 'A
common solution is to distinguish between 'forerunners'
(antichrists) and *the* antichrist. The 'antichrists' are pres-
ently with us; the 'antichrist' will appear at the end of
history. In this sense [Herman] Bavinck referred to the
antichristian powers throughout history, but believed that
one day these powers would be embodied in one kingdom
of the world, the apotheosis of apostasy. At any rate,
whether John is talking about antichrists or the antichrist,
the crux of his message is a warning. The central meaning
of the antichrist, according to John, is the great lie, the
denial that Jesus is the Christ."[3]

Berkouwer himself rejects Bavinck's view that the
antichrists are mere "forerunners." Berkouwer sees the
antichrist as an alarm signal to the church of all ages. This
does not answer the question, however, of whether the

antichrist of whom John warned was a specific person who had appeared in the first century. John's use of the masculine singular to refer to the antichrist militates against the antichrist being a vague institution, though it does not preclude it absolutely.

Alexander Ross strongly avows that the antichrist is not an institution but a *person*. He argues this point by linking John's antichrist with Paul's "man of lawlessness," who clearly is described in personal terms. "If, as is … almost certainly the case, John's Antichrist is to be identified with Paul's 'man of lawlessness' (2 Thess. 2:3)," Ross says, "the *personality* of Antichrist is clearly proved. . . . Outside the New Testament, we find writers like Justin Martyr, Irenaeus, Tertullian and Jerome dealing frequently with the subject of Antichrist, and all of these take Antichrist to be a person."[4]

The word *antichrist* is capable of more than one meaning or nuance, depending on how we understand the prefix *anti-*. The prefix normally means "against" and suggests someone who is in opposition to something. In this sense *antichrist* refers to someone who stands in opposition to Christ and who is his very antithesis. We generally use the English prefix *anti-* in the same manner to refer to someone or something that is against or in opposition to something else.

In Greek the prefix *anti-* can also be translated "in place of." That which is "anti" may function as a replacement or substitute for something. Theologians call this the *imitation motif.* So we might view the antichrist as a false Christ, or as one who seeks to usurp the rightful place of Christ. He is a fake or counterfeit Christ. Thus "imitation" refers to that which is not genuine but counterfeit.

It is not necessary to choose between these nuances of

the prefix. It is possible, if not probable, that the concept of antichrist contains both elements. At the very least the antichrist is one who stands and works "against" Christ. If, however, he also seeks to be a substitute for Christ, then the link to the man of lawlessness is even more enticing.

The Man of Lawlessness

Paul introduces the man of lawlessness in his Second Epistle to the Thessalonians.

> Let no one deceive you by any means; for that Day will not come unless the falling away comes first, and the man of sin is revealed, the son of perdition, who opposes and exalts himself above all that is called God or that is worshiped, so that he sits as God in the temple of God, showing himself that he is God. Do you not remember that when I was still with you I told you these things? And now you know what is restraining, that he may be revealed in his own time. For the mystery of lawlessness is already at work; only He who now restrains will do so until He is taken out of the way. And then the lawless one will be revealed, whom the Lord will consume with the breath of His mouth and destroy with the brightness of His coming. The coming of the lawless one is according to the working of Satan, with all power, signs, and lying wonders, and with all unrighteous deception among those who perish, because they did not receive the love of the truth, that they might be saved. And for this reason God will send them strong delusion, that they should believe the lie. ...
>
> *(2 Thess. 2:3–11)*

Paul's man of sin or lawlessness is often linked to or identified with the antichrist. If indeed both names refer to the same thing, then Paul has shed considerable light on the nature and character of the antichrist. First, the man of sin is identified as a man. This would tend to eliminate institutions from being the antichrist, except when an institution can be embodied in a single individual. The Reformers commonly considered the papacy as the antichrist, an institution that could be embodied in a particular pope. Likewise some have seen the government of the Roman Empire as the antichrist, which could be embodied in a specific emperor.

Second, the man of sin's lawless behavior has a strong religious dimension. He is "the son of perdition" who not only "opposes" God but also "exalts himself above ... God" (2 Thess. 2:3 – 4). Through a kind of self-apotheosis, this man claims for himself nothing short of deity. Paul does not call him "antichrist" here, but Paul does describe his activity in terms of being both *against* Christ and a *substitute* for Christ. Paul says the man of sin "sits as God in the temple of God" (2 Thess. 2:4). This suggests that this arrogant person will appear when the temple is in place, though conceivably the term *temple* merely designates a religious locale.

John Calvin, for example, had no problem seeing this as an allusion to the church. "This one word *[in the temple of God]* fully refutes the error or rather stupidity of those who hold the Pope to be the vicar of Christ on the ground that he has a settled residence in the Church, however he may conduct himself," Calvin writes. "Paul sets Antichrist in the very sanctuary of God. He is not an enemy from the outside but from the household of faith, and opposes Christ under the very name of Christ."[5]

Third, Paul comments on when the man of lawlessness will appear. Paul wrote to the Thessalonians that the "day of Christ" had not yet come. Paul said that day would not come until the apostasy (or falling away) occurs and the man of sin is revealed (2 Thess. 2:3).

What the apostle says next is the subject of great debate regarding the timing of the man of sin's appearance. Paul indicates that the "restrainer," whom his readers can identify, is present (2 Thess. 2:7). This one who restrains has been identified by modern commentators as the Roman government, Paul himself, and the Holy Spirit.

The latter is a favorite theory of some Dispensationalists who see in this text a thinly veiled reference to the rapture. That is, the rapture must occur before the antichrist is unleashed. For the antichrist to operate without restraint, the Holy Spirit must be first removed. For this to occur the Christian community must be physically removed from the earth, because as long as Christians are present in the world the Holy Spirit who indwells them is likewise present.

Whoever the restrainer is, he must be taken out of the way before the lawless one can be revealed. Paul does employ temporal terms similar to John's when he declares that "the mystery of lawlessness is *already at* work" (2 Thess. 2:7). Paul then states that "the lawless one" will be consumed by the Lord and destroyed "with the brightness of His coming" (2 Thess. 2:8). These statements imply that, though the man of lawlessness was already at work, he was not yet clearly manifest to Paul's contemporaries. This man's work would continue until Christ came and he was consumed.

Again the question of time-frame becomes critical. Was Paul speaking of a first-century person who would soon be made manifest and then be destroyed by the judgment-coming of Christ in A.D. 70? Or was Paul speaking of one who, though already at work in the first century, would not be fully revealed until sometime near the end of history as a precursor to the coming of Jesus?

Benjamin Breckinridge Warfield, cited by Gary DeMar, argues that Paul's man of lawlessness was a contemporary. Warfield writes:

> The withholding power is already present. Although the Man of Sin is not yet revealed, as a mystery his essential "lawlessness" is already working—"only until the present restrainer be removed from the midst." He expects him to sit in the "temple of God," which perhaps most naturally refers to the literal temple in Jerusalem, although the Apostle knew that the out-pouring of God's wrath on the Jews was close at hand (1 Thess. 2:16). And if we compare the description which the Apostle gives of him with our Lord's address on the Mount of Olives (Matt. 24), to which, as we have already hinted, Paul makes obvious allusion, it becomes at once in the highest degree probable that in the words, "he that exalteth himself against all that is called God, or is worshipped, so that he sitteth in the sanctuary of God showing himself that he is God," Paul can have nothing else in view than what our Lord described as "the abomination of desolation which was spoken of by Daniel the prophet, standing in the holy place" (Matt. 24:15); and this our Lord connects immediately with the beleaguering of Jerusalem (cf. Luke 21:20)[6]

DeMar argues that the apostasy of which Paul speaks (2 Thess. 2:3) was already in motion and was probably Jewish rather than Christian in nature. Paul is referring to the falling away of Jews who rejected Christ, not to an apostasy of the church at the end of history. Again DeMar quotes Warfield, who writes:

In this interpretation, the apostasy is obviously the great apostasy of the Jews, gradually filling up all these years and hasten-
ing to its completion in their destruction. That the Apostle
certainly had this rapidly completing apostasy in his mind in
the severe arraignment that he makes of the Jews in 1 Thess.
2:14–16, which reached its climax in the declaration that they
were continually filling up more and more full the measure of
their sins, until already the measure of God's wrath was prema-
turely … filled up against them and was hanging over them
like some laden thunder-cloud ready to burst and overwhelm
them, – adds an additional reason for supposing his reference
to be to this apostasy – above all others, "the" apostasy – in this
passage.[7]

In his treatment of 2 Thessalonians 2:3–11, J. B. Lightfoot
identifies a clear link between John's antichrist and Paul's
man of lawlessness. "One of the important features in this
description is the parallel drawn between Christ and the
adversary of Christ," Light-foot writes. "Both alike are 'revealed,' and to both alike the term 'mystery' is applied.
From this circumstance, and from the description given in
ver. 4 of his arrogant assumption, we cannot doubt that the
man of sin in St. Paul is identical with the Antichrist of St.
John, the preposition in the latter term expressing the idea
of antagonistic claims."[8]

The Beast

Nowhere in Scripture do we get such a graphic picture of a
wicked eschatological figure as the Apocalypse provides of
"the beast."

Then I stood on the sand of the sea. And I saw a beast rising up out of the sea, having seven heads and ten horns, and on his horns ten crowns, and on his heads a blasphemous name. Now the beast which I saw was like a leopard, his feet were like the feet of a bear, and his mouth like the mouth of a lion. And the dragon gave him his power, his throne, and great authority I saw one of his heads as if it had been mortally wounded, and his deadly wound was healed. And all the world marveled and followed the beast. So they worshiped the dragon who gave authority to the beast; and they worshiped the beast, saying, "Who is like the beast? Who is able to make war with him?" And he was given a mouth speaking great things and blasphemies, and he was given authority to continue for forty-two months. Then he opened his mouth in blasphemy against God, to blaspheme His name, His tabernacle, and those who dwell in heaven. And it was granted to him to make war with the saints and to overcome them. And authority was given him over every tribe, tongue, and nation. And all who dwell on the earth will worship him, whose names have not been written in the Book of Life of the Lamb slain from the foundation of the world. If anyone has an ear, let him hear. He who leads into captivity shall go into captivity; he who kills with the sword must be killed with the sword. Here is the patience and the faith of the saints.

Then I saw another beast coming up out of the earth, and he had two horns like a lamb and spoke like a dragon. And he exercises all the authority of the first beast in his presence, and causes the earth and those who dwell in it to worship the first beast, whose deadly wound was healed. He performs great signs, so that he even makes fire come down from heaven on the earth in the sight of men. And he deceives those who dwell on the earth by those signs which he was granted to do in the sight of the beast, telling those who dwell on the earth to make an image to the beast who was wounded by the sword and lived. He was granted power

Table 8.1   **The Antichrist**

Author	Description	Reference
John	As you have heard that the **Antichrist** is coming, even now many antichrists have come, by which we know that it is the last hour.	1 John 2:18
John	Every spirit that does not confess that Jesus Christ has come in the flesh is not of God. And this is the spirit of the **Antichrist,** which you have heard was coming, and is now already in the world.	1 John 4:1–4
Paul	That day will not come unless the falling away comes first, and the **man of sin** is revealed, the **son of perdition,** who opposes and exalts himself above all that is called God.	2 Thess. 2:3–4
Paul	Then the **lawless one** will be revealed.... The coming of the **lawless one** is according to the working of Satan, with all power, signs, and lying wonders.	2 Thess. 2:8–9
John	I saw a **beast** rising up out of the sea, having seven heads and ten horns.	Rev. 13:1
John	They worshiped the **beast,** saying, "Who is like the **beast**?". . . And he was given a mouth speaking great things and blasphemies.	Rev. 13:4–5
John	Authority was given [the **beast**] over every tribe, tongue, and nation. And all who dwell on the earth will worship him, whose names have not been written in the Book of Life.	Rev. 13:7

to give breath to the image of the beast, that the image of the beast should both speak and cause as many as would not worship the image of the beast to be killed. And he causes all, both small and great, rich and poor, free and slave, to receive a mark on their right hand or on their foreheads, and that no one may buy or sell except one who has the mark or the name of the beast, or the number of his name. Here is wisdom. Let him who has understanding calculate the number of the beast, for it is the number of a man: His number is 666.

Then I looked, and behold, a Lamb standing on Mount Zion, and with Him one hundred and forty-four thousand, having His Father's name written on their foreheads. ...

(Rev. 13:1—14:1)

Perhaps no biblical riddle has gripped and fascinated people more than this: who is the beast identified by the dreaded cryptogram 666. This riddle has fueled endless speculation throughout church history, resulting in a plethora of candidates. This person's number is referred to as "the mark of the beast."

As "bestial" as this figure is, he is clearly identified as a human being. "In general, more attention is given to the 'riddle' of this number than to the fact that it is 'a human number," Berkouwer says. "In other words, that all the subhumanity of the beast is still human, proceeding from among men, and setting itself up over against God and men."[9]

Kenneth L. Gentry Jr., who has written extensively regarding the dating of the Book of Revelation,[10] has also written an entire monograph concerning the identity of the beast.[11] Gentry concurs with Berkouwer that the beast whose number is 666 is a man, which excludes demonic beings, philosophical systems, political movements or empires, or anything other than a specific, individual, human person.

Even a cursory reading of Revelation 13 makes it clear that, like the antichrist and the man of lawlessness, the beast is an extremely evil and idolatrous person. Gentry adds that, since the beast possesses great "authority" (Rev. 13:5, 7) and wears ten crowns on his head (Rev. 13:1), he must be a political figure. (This, of course, does not preclude a religious figure who, in addition to his ecclesiastical authority, is also invested with political authority. The idea of separating civil and ecclesiastical authority has not been a consistent norm throughout history.)

Gentry also argues that the "name-number" (Rev. 13:18) must speak of someone who was a *contemporary* of John's. Gentry bases this primarily on the time-frame references in the Apocalypse (which we have already examined). "This principle alone," Gentry says, "will eliminate 99.9% of the suggestions by commentators."[12]

If the beast is one of John's contemporaries, Gentry argues, then it naturally follows that it is someone *relevant* to the recipients of John's letter. This further limits the candidates for the beast.

Gentry agrees with those commentators who affirm that John's portrait of the beast shifts between generic and specific imagery. The Beast is described as having seven heads (Rev. 13:1), which indicates a collective identity such as a kingdom or empire. Yet in this same context the beast is given a specific identity associated with the cryptic number 666 (Rev. 13:18).

Gentry points out that later in Revelation the seven heads are said to represent seven mountains (Rev. 17:9):

"Here is the mind which has wisdom: The seven heads are seven mountains on which the woman sits. There are also seven kings. Five have fallen, one is, and the other has not yet come. And when he comes, he must continue a short time. And the beast that was, and is not, is himself also the eighth,

and is of the seven, and is going to perdition. And the ten horns
which you saw are ten kings who have received no kingdom
as yet, but they receive authority for one hour as kings with the
beast. These are of one mind, and they will give their power
and authority to the beast."

(Rev. 17:9—13)

Some have argued that the seven-hilled city is Jerusalem,
identified with Babylon because of its spiritual harlotry.
The majority of commentators, however, see this as a reference to Rome, known widely as the "City on Seven Hills"
or, as it was called in antiquity, the *Septimontium*.

Notes to Chapter 13

[1] Alexander Ross, *The Epistles of James and John,* New International Commentary on the New Testament, ed. Ned B.
Stonehouse (Grand Rapids: Eerdmans, 1954), p. 168. See also
John Calvin's commentary on 1 John, and specifically his
comment on 2:18; the translation is Ross's.

[2] David Chilton, *Paradise Restored: A Biblical Theology of Dominion* (Fort Worth: Dominion, 1985), p. 111.

[3] G. C. Berkouwer, *The Return of Christ,* trans. James Van
Oosterom, Studies in Dogmatics (Grand Rapids: Eerdmans,
1972), p. 265. See Herman Bavinck, *Gereformeerde Dogmatiek,*
4th ed., 4 vols. (Kampen: Kok, 1928–30), 4:659. English translation in Bavinck, *The Last Things: Hope for This World and the
Next,* ed. John Bolt, trans. John Vriend (Grand Rapids: Baker,
1996), pp. 113–14.

[4] Ross, *The Epistles of James and John,* p. 169 (n. 2).

[5] John Calvin, *The Epistles of Paul the Apostle to the Romans and to
the Thessalonians,* trans. Ross Mackenzie, ed. David W.
Torrance and Thomas F. Torrance (Grand Rapids: Eerdmans,
1961), p. 402.

6 Benjamin Breckinridge Warfield, "The Prophecies of St.
   Paul," in Warfield, *Biblical Doctrines* (1929; reprint, Grand
   Rapids: Baker, 1981), pp. 609–10. Also in Warfield, *Biblical and
   Theological Studies,* ed. Samuel G. Craig (Philadelphia: Presby-
   terian and Reformed, 1952), p. 472. Quoted in Gary DeMar,
   *Last Days Madness: The Folly of Trying to Predict When Christ
   Will Return* (Brentwood, Tenn.: Wolgemuth & Hyatt, 1991),
   p. 159.

7 Warfield, "The Prophecies of St. Paul" (1929), p. 612; (1952),
   p. 474. Quoted in Gary DeMar, *Last Days Madness,* pp. 159–
   60.

8 J. B. Lightfoot, *Notes on Epistles of St. Paul: 1–2 Thessalonians,
   1 Corinthians 1–7, Romans 1–7, Ephesians 1:1–14,* ed. J. R.
   Harmer (1895; reprint, Grand Rapids: Baker, 1980), p. 111.

9 Berkouwer, *The Return of Christ,* p. 279.

10 Kenneth L. Gentry Jr., *Before Jerusalem Fell: Dating the Book of
   Revelation: An Exegetical and Historical Argument for a Pre-A.D.
   70 Composition* (Tyler, Tex.: Institute for Christian Economics,
   1989).

11 Kenneth L. Gentry Jr., *The Beast of Revelation* (Tyler, Tex.:
   Institute for Christian Economics, 1989).

12 Gentry, *The Beast of Revelation,* p. 10.

one person
can call for change ...

one million people
can become
a movement for change

evangelical alliance
uniting to change society

Website: www.eauk.org Email: info@eauk.org Tel: (020) 7207 2100

Registered Charity No 212325

growing
in the
Word vouchers

£1 off *A Cop for Christ*

This 'growing *in the* Word' voucher £1 is redeemable against the purchase of *A Cop for Christ (Hodder & Stoughton)* in all bookshops participating in the promotion. Offer valid until 30th June 2001. Voucher cannot be exchanged for cash or any other merchandise.

£1 off *A Time to Jump*

This 'growing *in the* Word' voucher £1 is redeemable against the purchase of *A Time to Jump paperback (HarperCollins)* in all bookshops participating in the promotion. Offer valid until 30th June 2001. Voucher cannot be exchanged for cash or any other merchandise.

£2 off *The God Catchers*

This 'growing *in the* Word' voucher £2 is redeemable against the purchase of *The God Catchers (Word)* in all bookshops participating in the promotion. Offer valid until 30th June 2001. Voucher cannot be exchanged for cash or any other merchandise.

£1 off *Faithworks*

This 'growing *in the* Word' voucher £1 is redeemable against the purchase of *Faithworks (Kingsway)* in all bookshops participating in the promotion. Offer valid until 30th June. Voucher cannot be exchanged for cash or any other merchandise.

growing *in the* *Word* vouchers

£2 off *Fresh Power*

This 'growing *in the* *Word*' voucher £2 is redeemable against the purchase of *Fresh Power (Zondervan)* in all bookshops participating in the promotion. Offer valid until 30th June 2001. Voucher cannot be exchanged for cash or any other merchandise.

£3 off *The Mark*

This 'growing *in the* *Word*' voucher £3 is redeemable against the purchase of *The Mark hardback (Tyndale)* in all bookshops participating in the promotion. Offer valid until 30th June 2001. Voucher cannot be exchanged for cash or any other merchandise.

£2 off *A New Chapter*

This 'growing *in the* *Word*' voucher £2 is redeemable against the purchase of *A New Chapter (Paternoster)* in all bookshops participating in the promotion. Offer valid until 30th June 2001. Voucher cannot be exchanged for cash or any other merchandise.

£1 off *Light from a Dark Star*

This 'growing *in the* *Word*' voucher £1 is redeemable against the purchase of *Light from a Dark Star (Scripture Union)* in all bookshops participating in the promotion. Offer valid until 30th June 2001. Voucher cannot be exchanged for cash or any other merchandise.

growing
in the
Word vouchers

£2 off *Are You Listening*

This 'growing *in the* Word' voucher £2 is redeemable against the purchase of *Are You Listening (Kevin Mayhew)* in all bookshops participating in the promotion. Offer valid until 30th June 2001. Voucher cannot be exchanged for cash or any other merchandise.

£2 off *Victory Over the Darkness*

This 'growing *in the* Word' voucher £2 is redeemable against the purchase of *Victory Over the Darkness (Monarch)* in all bookshops participating in the promotion. Offer valid until 30th June 2001. Voucher cannot be exchanged for cash or any other merchandise.

£3 off *The Hand of God*

This 'growing *in the* Word' voucher £3 is redeemable against the purchase of *The Hand of God hardback (Moody)* in all bookshops participating in the promotion. Offer valid until 30th June 2001. Voucher cannot be exchanged for cash or any other merchandise.

£1 off *Dear Paul*

This 'growing *in the* Word' voucher £1 is redeemable against the purchase of *Dear Paul (BRF)* in all bookshops participating in the promotion. Offer valid until 30th June 2001. Voucher cannot be exchanged for cash or any other merchandise.

growing *in the* **Word** vouchers

£6 *off* NLT Living Water

This 'growing *in the* **Word**' voucher £6 is redeemable against the purchase of *NLT Living Water hardback (Tyndale)* in all bookshops participating in the promotion. Offer valid until 30th June 2001. Voucher cannot be exchanged for cash or any other merchandise.

£2 *off* Message of the Living God

This 'growing *in the* **Word**' voucher £2 is redeemable against the purchase of *Message of the Living God (IVP)* in all bookshops participating in the promotion. Offer valid until 30th June 2001. Voucher cannot be exchanged for cash or any other merchandise.

£1 *off* No Compromise

This 'growing *in the* **Word**' voucher £1 is redeemable against the purchase of *No Compromise (Harvest House)* in all bookshops participating in the promotion. Offer valid until 30th June 2001. Voucher cannot be exchanged for cash or any other merchandise.

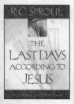

£2 *off* Last Days According to Jesus

This 'growing *in the* **Word**' voucher £2 is redeemable against the purchase of *Last Days According to Jesus (Baker)* in all bookshops participating in the promotion. Offer valid until 30th June 2001. Voucher cannot be exchanged for cash or any other merchandise.